MIDDLESBROUGH
On This Day

MIDDLESBROUGH
On This Day

*History, Facts & Figures
from Every Day of the Year*

**GORDON REES, TOSH WARWICK
AND SHAUN WILSON**

First published by Pitch Publishing, 2024

Pitch Publishing
9 Donnington Park,
85 Birdham Road,
Chichester, West Sussex,
PO20 7AJ
www.pitchpublishing.co.uk
info@pitchpublishing.co.uk

A CIP catalogue record is available for this book
from the British Library.

ISBN 978 1 80150 665 6

Printed and bound in the UK on FSC® certified paper in line
with our continuing commitment to ethical business practices,
sustainability and the environment.

Typesetting and origination by Pitch Publishing

Printed and bound by CPI Antony Rowe, UK

RICHARD PIERS RAYNER DEPICTS THE FIRST LEAGUE GOAL AT AYRESOME PARK IN 1903

INTRODUCTION

The history of Middlesbrough Football Club dates back to 1876 and, like so many other clubs across the country, has its origins in the town's local cricket club coming together to find a suitable sporting pursuit to keep the team active and together out of season. Fast approaching the 150th anniversary of the formation of the town's premier football club, the Boro are synonymous with the town and have arguably usurped the iron, steel and bridge-building industries as the key identifying characteristic for which the 'Ironopolis' was best known into the 1980s.

Middlesbrough have not been blessed with an array of national honours or top-flight titles, listing only two FA Amateur Cups in 1895 and 1898 at amateur level and a League Cup win in 2004 since as their major national honours. Yet a lack of trophy wins should not be aligned with a lack of success. In fact, the club has at times far surpassed all expectations and famously fought back from the brink of extinction in 1986 to enjoy successive promotions led by Bruce Rioch.

Boro have also contributed to the rich tapestry of British football by producing or listing among their number record-breakers and pivotal figures in the history of the beautiful game. Ayresome Park, opened in 1903, was the first English ground designed by the famed football stadium architect Archibald Leitch. In 1905, Middlesbrough were responsible for breaking the transfer record in signing the world's first £1,000 footballer as Alf Common switched Wearside for Teesside. Into the interwar years, George Camsell smashed the Football League record for goals in a season when he hammered home 59 league goals during the 1926/27 campaign, and the same player went on to become England's record goals-to-games goalscorer with an astonishing 18 scored in nine appearances for the national side. The club's record goalscorer was one of dozens of Middlesbrough players who went on to play international football for the home nations, including Great Britain and England captain George Hardwick, football's 'Golden Boy' Wilf Mannion, the controversial but brilliant Brian Clough, Boro's own Stewart Downing, defensive lynchpin Gary Pallister and the Auld Enemy's superb Graeme Souness. Ex-Boro bosses Steve McClaren and Gareth Southgate went on to take over the Three

Lions, while Jack Charlton began his management career at Boro by crafting the famous 'Charlton's Champions' side and later went on to manage the Republic of Ireland at two World Cups.

Since the 1990s, Boro have enjoyed some of the most dramatic and successful times in the club's history. They moved into what was at the time the largest new stadium built since the Second World War and boldly led the way in bringing some of the world's leading players – including Brazilian Footballer of the Year Juninho – to England's shores. They were the first club to reach three consecutive major English domestic finals inside 12 months, albeit losing them all amid the agony of relegation following a controversial points deduction. In 2004 they finally brought major silverware back to Teesside as Gareth Southgate lifted the League Cup at the Millennium Stadium in Cardiff.

There are also the less-well-known moments in the club's story that nevertheless played an important part in footballers' careers and, more importantly, are treasured memories or played a key part in the footballing DNA of generations of Boro supporters who cheered on the boys in white and blue from the main stand at the Linthorpe Road Ground, sang their hearts out for the lads in red from the Holgate End, and jumped out of their favourite seat at the Riverside Stadium as Massimo Maccarone's goal sent Boro to the UEFA Cup Final.

In bringing together the famous matches, the stories of star names, incredible achievements, agonising failures and some of the quirky and less-known moments from Boro's story, this book – day-by-day – attempts to present a flavour of the various pieces that come together to form the history of Middlesbrough Football Club.

ACKNOWLEDGEMENTS

Middlesbrough Football Club has been a source of passion and intrigue for many supporters and writers over the years and this book would not have been possible without the work of many who have actively contributed to this publication, and those whose work we have drawn on extensively in revealing the story of the Boro day-by-day.

The match reports and daily Boro updates found in the pages of the *North-Eastern Daily Gazette* (and its successors) and *Sports Gazette* have been indispensable. The reports by 'Old Bird' delivered from the main stand at the Linthorpe Road Ground, Captain Jack's captivating coverage of the majesty of Mannion, and Cliff Mitchell's chronicling of the fall to the Third Division and the rise back to the top tier under the leadership of Stan Anderson and Jack Charlton have helped bring colour, context and character to raw and sometimes drab match statistics, transfer fees and annual accounts.

We are also indebted to numerous contemporary contributors who have either knowingly or unknowingly helped bring this book to print through their work in keeping today's Boro fans up to date with the day's news or keeping the club's history alive. These include a host of *Evening Gazette* journalists past and present who have been at the heart of bringing the stories from the pitch to print, including the likes of Eric Paylor, Philip Tallentire, Dominic Shaw and Anthony Vickers, whose match reports, transfer exclusives, manager interviews and frequent evocative and eloquent retreats to that the Boro of yesteryear have been seminal texts for fans. The decades-long contribution of Gordon Cox in delivering the latest from the club across various mediums has also helped reveal fascinating tales from Ayresome Park to the Riverside, while the match commentaries of the late, great Ali Brownlee – some quoted in the book – have transmitted the delight and despair of a life of loving Middlesbrough to the masses. Various Boro history publications have also proven invaluable, in particular the works of many of those already mentioned as well as many others including, but not limited to, Dave Allan, Graham Bell, Adrian Bevington, Harry Glasper, David Harnby, Tim Hetherington, Chris Kershaw, Harry Pearson, Alan Spence, Paul Thompson and John Wilson.

Multiple extracts and photographs featured in this book have been made available from various newspaper collections, archives and personal papers and we are grateful to the *Gazette*'s Craig Johns, *Fly Me To The Moon* editor Robert Nichols, *The Northern Echo*'s Chris Lloyd, Middlesbrough Libraries, Middlesbrough Museums, Middlesbrough FC, Teesside Archives, the Boro Shirt Museum's Mark Davies and Jamie Fox, artist Richard Piers Rayner, Helen Camsell, John Culley, Colin Galloway, Harry Greenmon and Jed Mawson. We would also like to thank all those who we may have omitted in error from these acknowledgements.

Lastly, we would like to dedicate this book to all Boro fans who have supported the club through thick and thin from those early days at Albert Park to the present day at the Riverside Stadium. Up the Boro!

Tosh Warwick, Gordon Rees and Shaun Wilson
June 2024

ABOUT THE AUTHORS

Dr Tosh Warwick attended his first Boro match in April 1988 in a 6-0 win over Sheffield United at Ayresome Park. Tosh has authored a number of books and articles on Middlesbrough history and is a regular contributor to the club's official matchday programme.

Gordon Rees attended his first Boro match in 1971 and has supported Boro for over five decades. He is an avid collector of Middlesbrough FC ephemera and has shared his extensive knowledge of Boro's history across several platforms.

Shaun Wilson is a long-term contributor to Middlesbrough FC's official matchday programme and collector of Boro memorabilia. Shaun is co-author of several books on the club's history, including recent publications on matchday programmes.

MIDDLESBROUGH
On This Day

JANUARY

1st JANUARY 1927

A crowd of 26,163 at Ayresome Park witnessed Middlesbrough hammer Port Vale 5-2 courtesy of three goals from George Camsell, a Billy Pease strike and an own goal as Boro continued their push for promotion to the top flight. Camsell's hat-trick made it ten goals in eight days for the Middlesbrough forward en route to a record haul of 59 league goals in a season.

1st JANUARY 1936

Goal ace George Camsell scored his penultimate Football League hat-trick in a 3-1 win over West Bromwich Albion at Ayresome Park, on the way to scoring 28 goals in 38 league appearances.

1st JANUARY 1959

A brace from the second tier's top goalscorer, Brian Clough, and a strike by Scotland international Willie Fernie – his first for the club after a switch from Glasgow Celtic – were enough for Boro to see off Huddersfield Town 3-1 at Ayresome Park.

1st JANUARY 1997

Aged 39 years, 11 months and 21 days, Bryan Robson turned out in a 2-0 loss to Arsenal at Highbury to become the club's then oldest player – a record that stood until January 2019 when Dimi Konstantopoulos appeared at 40 years and 38 days. While Dimi had little to do in a 5-0 win over Peterborough United, Robson's final professional outing saw him at the heart of the action to the extent that the *Evening Gazette*'s Eric Paylor considered the former England skipper's performance worthy of the man of the match award.

1st JANUARY 2002

Gianluca Festa's second-half goal against Everton at the Riverside ended a run of four straight defeats for Steve McClaren's struggling side as they moved three points clear of the final relegation spot.

2nd JANUARY 1937

Young ex-South Bank St Peter's boy Wilf Mannion made his Boro debut in a 2-2 draw with Portsmouth, stepping in as a last-minute replacement for the injured Cliff Chadwick. The local newspaper report noted that the new man 'lacks a little speed at the moment' but felt, 'Mannion appears to have more than "a chance" of making good later on. This outing will have done him good.'

2ND JANUARY 1989

Peter Davenport, a £700,000 record signing from Manchester United the previous year, scored his first goal for the club in a 1-0 win over his former employers in front of a season-high 24,411 gate at Ayresome Park. The win was Boro's first victory in the league since mid-November and ended a seven-game winless run in the First Division, while the result brought Alex Ferguson's men back down to earth after a 3-1 win against Liverpool at Old Trafford the previous day.

2ND JANUARY 1995

A bumper crowd at Ayresome Park was left disappointed as Boro's match with Barnsley was abandoned at half-time owing to an icy pitch, with the home side leading 2-1. The fixture was the last to be abandoned at the club's home of 92 years. To make matters worse for the Boro faithful, the rescheduled game ended 1-1 with ex-Middlesbrough man Andy Payton scoring against his former employer after Jaime Moreno had scored his first league goal for the club.

3RD JANUARY 1981

The FA Cup third round brought a long-distance journey to the Vetch Field where Boro turned on the style to defeat Swansea City 5-0. The match is best remembered for Northern Ireland schemer Terry Cochrane's stunning overhead kick that was one of the goals of the season.

3RD JANUARY 2009

Boro edged past non-league Barrow in the FA Cup third round courtesy of a 2-1 win at the Riverside. Afonso Alves's brace put the home side in the comfort zone before Jason Walker scored with ten minutes remaining to set up a grandstand finish and bring hope to the 7,000 travelling Bluebirds supporters.

4TH JANUARY 1997

Over 2,500 Chester City fans filled the away end at the Riverside Stadium for the FA Cup third round tie but had little to cheer as Boro ran out 6-0 winners, with the visitors' Kevin Noteman missing a penalty at 5-0. Fabrizio Ravanelli (two), Craig Hignett – who was later dismissed – Neil Cox, Mikkel Beck and Phil Stamp were on the scoresheet in an impressive win that proved to be the start of the most successful FA Cup run in the club's history.

5TH JANUARY 1907

One-time record £750 signing Steve Bloomer scored four as the Teessiders gunned down Woolwich Arsenal, running out 5-3 winners at Ayresome Park to gain two vital points in their battle against the drop.

6TH JANUARY 2024

High-flying Aston Villa struggled to overcome Championship Middlesbrough in the FA Cup third round at the Riverside until a late Matty Cash goal settled the tie for the visitors in the 87th minute.

7TH JANUARY 1975

David Armstrong scored an 89th-minute penalty to spare top-flight Boro's blushes against non-league Wycombe Wanderers in an FA Cup third round replay at Ayresome Park and set up a clash with north-east rivals Sunderland in the next round.

8TH JANUARY 2011

Boro were stunned by third-tier Burton Albion at the Pirelli Stadium after the Brewers fought back from a goal down to win 2-1 to progress to the next round of the FA Cup. Gary O'Neil's free kick looked to have ensured the Teessiders' passage to the next round but Shaun Harrad equalised in the 82nd minute before grabbing a 94th-minute winner on a day of shocks that saw north-east rivals Newcastle United dumped out of the competition by Stevenage Borough and Sunderland lose at home to Notts County.

9TH JANUARY 1926

Jimmy McClelland scored all five of the home team's goals as Boro sent Leeds United crashing out of the FA Cup with a 5-1 win in the first competitive meeting between the two sides.

10TH JANUARY 1978

Prized-asset and want-away midfielder Graeme Souness finally completed his move to Bob Paisley's Liverpool for £352,000 – a record transfer fee between Football League clubs. The move followed a stand-off between manager John Neal and the fiery Scot, who was keen to cement his place in the Scotland World Cup squad by catching the eye of national team manager Ally MacLeod with impressive performances for his new club.

11TH JANUARY 2003

The enigmatic Alen Bokšić was substituted after 71 minutes in his final appearance for Middlesbrough with his side trailing 2-0 to visitors Southampton. Goals in the last 15 minutes by substitutes Noel Whelan and Massimo Maccarone – who replaced the Croatian in attack – rescued a point for the home side. The former Lazio man's final appearance for Boro epitomised a frustrating stay on Teesside for a player who, on his day, showed that he was among the best strikers in Europe yet all too often missed out through injury. Nevertheless, his goal return of 22 in 68 appearances over two and a half seasons helped Boro avoid relegation across two difficult years.

12TH JANUARY 1952

Wilf Mannion's two goals were not enough to ensure Boro progressed to the FA Cup fourth round at the first time of asking as Derby County secured a replay in a 2-2 draw at Ayresome Park.

13TH JANUARY 1973

Stan Anderson's Middlesbrough crashed out of the FA Cup at Plymouth Argyle, leaving the Boro manager questioning his own future as his side struggled in league and cups.

14TH JANUARY 1997

Boro were deducted three points by the Premier League's disciplinary commission as punishment for calling off the match scheduled to be played at Ewood Park the previous month owing to illness in the squad. The club were ordered to pay a £50,000 fine and the associated costs of the commission, as well as to play a rescheduled fixture with Blackburn Rovers.

14TH JANUARY 2020

Middlesbrough's FA Cup campaign was brought to an end with a 2-1 defeat on their first visit to the Tottenham Hotspur Stadium. The Londoners raced into a two-goal lead before George Saville pulled one back for the visitors. Rudy Gestede had a chance late on to equalise but failed to convert from eight yards out.

15TH JANUARY 1997

Teessiders reacted with anger to the three-point deduction by the Premier League with the front-page headline of the *Evening Gazette* reading 'The POINT we want to make' as 'enraged Boro fans today cried foul on the draconian decision of the Premier League's punishment panel'.

16TH JANUARY 1929

Boro's FA Cup tie with Walsall was called off despite the best efforts of 'a large number of unemployed' to clear the six-inch-deep snow from the Ayresome Park turf. The match was called off at 2.15pm with some 10,000 supporters outside the gates awaiting a decision on whether it would go ahead.

16TH JANUARY 1998

Newspapers across the country reported stay-away midfielder Emerson's accusations that the club had let him down on a new contract offer as he prepared to complete a £4.25m move to Tenerife. The accusations followed Steve Gibson speaking out at his bitter disappointment at the former Porto man's failure to return to the club after a Christmas break. Speaking several years later, Emerson admitted that he made a mistake in the way that he departed the club and the Brazilian is still remembered fondly by many Boro fans.

16TH JANUARY 2007

One of the most remarkable FA Cup ties in Boro's history ended in the home team's favour at the Riverside as they triumphed 4-3 against Hull City. After leading 3-0 courtesy of a first-half Seb Hines goal followed by Mark Viduka and Yakubu strikes early in the second half, Boro conceded twice within the space of four minutes. Viduka restored the two-goal cushion before Andy Dawson added his second goal of the match in a frantic second half that brought six goals in 20 minutes.

17TH JANUARY 1995

The third-round replay against Swansea City proved to be the final FA Cup match to be played at Ayresome Park. Having drawn 1-1 at the Vetch Field ten days earlier, the Swans claimed a shock win through goals from Steve Torpey and Dave Penney, with John Hendrie's reply not enough to keep Boro's cup dreams alive. It was the second season in a row that Boro had exited the cup to Welsh opposition, having been knocked out by Cardiff City in a third-round replay at Ayresome Park the previous season.

18TH JANUARY 2002

Diego Forlán flew into Gatwick Airport as Boro hoped to complete a deal for the Uruguayan international. However, the *Evening Gazette*'s back-page headline instead read 'Forlán at the Final Hurdle' as it was revealed that 'Boro were today rocked as goal-getting target Diego Forlán snubbed Teesside to join Manchester United', with the young forward declaring, 'We are flying to Manchester and I am signing for Manchester United.'

19TH JANUARY 1974

Bolivian international forward Jaime Moreno was born in Santa Cruz. Signed in 1994 after playing for his nation at the 1994 World Cup, the first Bolivian to play in the Premier League struggled to make an impression on Teesside in two spells at the club. Moreno went on to have a highly successful career in Major Soccer League with D.C. United, breaking the league goalscoring record when notching his 109th MLS goal against New York Red Bulls in 2010 and winning multiple individual and team accolades.

20TH JANUARY 1998

The Guardian reported that Boro target Dion Dublin had rejected a £5m switch to Teesside from Coventry City despite Bryan Robson's insistence that his former Manchester United team-mate simply wanted time to think over the move to the north-east.

20TH JANUARY 2004

A well-worked second-half strike by Juninho gave Boro a 1-0 League Cup semi-final first leg win at Highbury to hand Arsenal's 'Invincibles' their first domestic defeat over 90 minutes of the season. The Teessiders might have had a more significant advantage going into the second leg but Juninho's first-half effort struck the inside of the post and Joseph-Désiré Job missed two good chances in the closing stages.

21ST JANUARY 1929

Middlesbrough triumphed 5-1 against Walsall in their on-off FA Cup fourth round replay which had already been postponed twice. George Camsell and Billy Pease each grabbed a brace and Owen Williams added Boro's other goal to book a tie with Walsall's local rivals West Bromwich Albion.

22ND JANUARY 1928

Boro's in-form marksman George Camsell faced a race against time when he received a late call-up to the England trial match at The Hawthorns the following day. The ex-Durham City man had to depart by rail at 7am from Middlesbrough and then head in a taxi to West Bromwich Albion's home ground. Unsurprisingly, he failed to impress and instead it was Dixie Dean, on the opposing side, who grabbed the attention of the selectors with a hat-trick.

21ST JANUARY 1929 – BILLY PEASE WAS ON TARGET AGAINST WALSALL IN THE FA CUP (CULLEY COLLECTION)

22ND JANUARY 1962

Stephen Pears, widely considered one of the best goalkeepers in the club's history, was born in Brandon. Pears initially joined Boro on loan from Manchester United in 1983 before returning on a permanent deal in 1985. He went on to play 339 league games in a total of 424 appearances that included four promotions, three relegations, one Wembley appearance and an England call-up, although injury would ultimately prevent the stopper playing for the national side.

23RD JANUARY 1915

Middlesbrough's reserves faced criticism in the local press after recording a remarkable 19-1 victory over Skelton Celtic in the North Riding Senior Cup at Ayresome Park. One local sport journalist described the score as absurd and contended that 'a score of four or five to one would have amply served the purpose in these anxious times, when small clubs meet with sufficient rebuffs to discourage them … [there] is no reason why they should be so humbled as to practically be ridiculed'.

23RD JANUARY 2024

Morgan Rogers scored his final Boro goal as Middlesbrough were trounced 6-1 by Chelsea in the League Cup semi-final second leg at Stamford Bridge. Boro's 1-0 aggregate lead from the first leg was wiped out by a Jonny Howson own goal after 15 minutes before Enzo Fernández, Axel Disasi and Cole Palmer added further goals before half-time. As the game petered out, Palmer and Noni Madueke made it six for the Londoners before the Aston Villa-bound attacker scored a consolation goal with two minutes left on the clock.

24TH JANUARY 2015

On-loan Chelsea striker Patrick Bamford and Spaniard Kike were the Boro heroes as they humbled Premier League champions Manchester City at the Etihad. The 2-0 FA Cup fourth round win for Championship Boro brought the sixth – and most surprising – clean sheet in seven games for Aitor Karanka's side. It was the second successive season that Manchester City had exited the tournament to a second-tier side, having crashed out to holders Wigan Athletic at the quarter-final stage in the previous campaign.

25TH JANUARY 1975

Boro cruised past Sunderland into the fifth round of the FA Cup in front of the *Match of the Day* cameras. A common feature of the tournament during the period, both teams donned their away kit with Boro in their now iconic blue-and-black-striped shirts and Sunderland in white. Despite Sunderland taking the lead after intercepting a rare misplaced pass by Graeme Souness, the midfielder soon made amends with an assist for fellow Scot Bobby Murdoch, who equalised in front of the Holgate. Into the second half, David Mills was felled by the Sunderland goalkeeper and John Hickton, complete with a trademark long penalty run-up, tucked the resultant spot kick into the corner of the net. As the Mackems pushed for an equaliser, Boro countered and Mills was felled in the box once again. Hickton coolly added his second from the spot to make sure of the club's first FA Cup win over their Roker rivals.

26TH JANUARY 2002

Noel Whelan and substitute Andy Campbell scored to see Steve McClaren's side dump Manchester United out of the FA Cup in the fourth round in a midday TV clash that attracted a crowd of just 17,624 to the Riverside. The tie looked to be heading for a replay at Old Trafford until former Leeds man Whelan struck in the 84th minute, and Campbell added another with a minute remaining to give the home side a 2-0 win that set up a fifth-round Riverside date with Blackburn Rovers.

27TH JANUARY 1896

After deliberation lasting several months, the approach from the chairman of Middlesbrough's Baseball Club for Middlesbrough Football Club to run the former was declined. Middlesbrough's directors also decided that the use of the Linthorpe Road Ground for baseball would no longer be permitted, although the decision was eventually overturned but with numerous caveats.

28TH JANUARY 1978

Boro manager John Neal gave promising 17-year-old Australian Craig Johnston his debut as Everton took on Boro at Ayresome Park in the FA Cup fourth round. A player derided by previous boss Jack Charlton, Johnston had impressed in the club's reserves to earn the number ten shirt vacated by the suspended Tony McAndrew. Boro led 3-0 with goals from John Mahoney and a brace from David Mills before the Merseysiders looked to stage an unlikely comeback but the home side hung on for a 3-2 victory.

CRAIG JOHNSTON MADE HIS DEBUT AGAINST EVERTON AS A TEENAGER (GORDON REES)

29TH JANUARY 1983

After struggling to dispose of non-league Bishop's Stortford after a replay in the FA Cup third round, Boro – languishing in the lower echelons of the Second Division – were handed a home draw against Notts County that attracted the biggest crowd of the season to date at Ayresome Park. A Ray Hankin goal and Kevin Beattie's penalty – Boro's final FA Cup penalty scored at the famous old ground – proved enough to seal a victory that sent the majority of the 17,114 crowd home happy.

30TH JANUARY 1982

Stephen Bell made his debut at home to a Southampton side that included Kevin Keegan and returning Boro favourite David Armstrong. Having impressed manager Bobby Murdoch in training, the slim-built, blond-haired winger became the then youngest Boro debutant aged just 16 years and 323 days. Without a league win since 26th September and rooted at the foot of the top-flight table, Murdoch's side were felled by a solitary goal from Keegan as the Teessiders headed for relegation.

30TH JANUARY 1988

A colossal series of FA Cup fourth round ties with Everton began with a visit to the reigning champions. Bruce Rioch's Second Division promotion-chasers fell behind in the first half to a Graeme Sharp goal but battled back after the interval as Paul Kerr converted a Stuart Ripley cross. Everton had a chance to secure their progress to the next round but Stephen Pears saved well to take the tie to a replay at Ayresome Park.

30TH JANUARY 1990

A 2-1 Zenith Data Systems Northern Final first leg win at Villa Park put Boro in the driving seat as they sought a first appearance at Wembley. Torrential rain poured down in Birmingham and Boro fell behind to a Paul Birch goal in the 13th minute but Bernie Slaven restored parity two minutes later. The tie appeared to be heading for a draw until Mark Brennan scored a stunning last-minute winner from outside the box following a short free kick.

31ST JANUARY 2003

Bolton Wanderers striker Michael Ricketts completed a late transfer deadline day move to Middlesbrough, joining new recruits Malcolm Christie and Chris Riggott, who both moved to Teesside from Derby County.

DAVID ARMSTRONG, PICTURED HERE DURING HIS BORO PLAYING DAYS, RETURNED TO AYRESOME PARK WITH SOUTHAMPTON (THE GAZETTE)

31ST JANUARY 2006

Emanuel Pogatetz and Stuart Parnaby proved to be the unlikely goal heroes as Boro trounced a sorry Sunderland 3-0 at the Stadium of Light. Leading 2-0 at half-time, Jimmy Floyd Hasselbaink added to the relegation-bound Mackems' woes with a rifled shot following a delightful ball from Gaizka Mendieta.

31ST JANUARY 2008

Boro paid a club-record £12.7m for Brazilian international Afonso Alves as they looked to boost their attacking threat. Signed from Dutch side Heerenveen, Alves had lit up the Eredivisie and topped the previous season's scoring charts with 34 goals in 31 games.

MIDDLESBROUGH
On This Day

FEBRUARY

1ST FEBRUARY 1986

Lennie Lawrence's Charlton Athletic inflicted a devastating loss on Willie Maddren's bewildered Boro as the Teessiders' prospects of steering away from relegation took another blow. Without a win all year and out of the FA Cup, the 3-1 home defeat to the Addicks came in front of just 4,695 fans at Ayresome Park. The loss left Maddren's charges languishing in 20th place ahead of an Arctic blast that caused chaos to fixtures across the country and meant Boro would not play another league game until March. For Maddren, it proved to be his last match in charge with the former Boro defender departing after the game by 'mutual consent'.

2ND FEBRUARY 1974

Nottingham Forest stunned Jack Charlton's Second Division table-toppers at the City Ground as they hammered the visitors 5-1. Alan Foggon scored Boro's goal in the defeat, which was followed by an 11-match unbeaten run.

3RD FEBRUARY 1986

Bruce Rioch, appointed first-team coach the previous month, stepped up as manager on a temporary basis following the departure of Willie Maddren. The 38-year-old former Scottish international said, 'I relish the fresh challenge. Middlesbrough can avoid relegation if we show a positive attitude,' while stressing, 'I would like to make it clear I am very sad over the departure of Willie Maddren.'

3RD FEBRUARY 1988

A topsy-turvy FA Cup third round replay ended 2-2 at Ayresome Park as league champions Everton narrowly escaped an upset. Going into the final minute of normal time, Everton led through a Dave Watson goal. However, Tony Mowbray scored a flying header in the dying seconds to take the tie to extra time. Boro led nine minutes into extra time after substitute Alan Kernaghan bundled home from close range. With seconds remaining, the home side were denied a famous win when a combination of Trevor Steven and Tony Mowbray competed for a cross and the ball was directed beyond the despairing dive of Stephen Pears.

4TH FEBRUARY 1998

A Craig Hignett opener and Paul Merson brace returned Boro to the summit of the First Division as they powered to a 3-0 Riverside win over struggling Tranmere Rovers.

BRUCE RIOCH STEPPED IN AS MANAGER FOLLOWING THE DEPARTURE OF WILLIE MADDREN (THE GAZETTE)

5TH FEBRUARY 1985

Boro's then-lowest league attendance at Ayresome Park saw just 3,477 turn out with the gloom and despair at the club evident as gates plummeted. Those who were present witnessed another defeat for the home side as Oldham Athletic headed back across the Pennines with three points after a 2-1 win, with debutant substitute Stuart Ripley unable to change the home side's fortunes.

6TH FEBRUARY 1915

As the first team were hammered 4-0 at Turf Moor, the reserves' North Eastern League clash with Houghton Rovers at Ayresome Park produced arguably the most one-sided game in the ground's history. England international George Elliott scored ten goals in a 15-0 win against the County Durham side who played with only eight men.

6TH FEBRUARY 1971

Promotion-chasing Boro hammered Norwich City at Ayresome Park to climb into sixth place and just three points behind leaders Hull City. Eric McMordie was the provider as the home side raced into a two-goal lead in the opening quarter of an hour thanks to goals from Derrick Downing and John Hickton. Hugh McIlmoyle headed Boro's third from a Gordon Jones cross to open up a commanding first-half lead. Hickton added a second after the break before Joe Laidlaw completed the scoring.

7TH FEBRUARY 1979

Boro's Terry Cochrane was helpless to stop England trouncing Northern Ireland 4-0 at Wembley in a European Championship qualifier between the two sides.

8TH FEBRUARY 1927

An extraordinary clash at struggling Grimsby Town produced an 11-goal thriller as Boro underlined their promotion credentials. George Camsell scored a hat-trick, Billy Birrell added a brace and Jimmy McClelland and Jesse Thomas Williams notched the other goals to help Middlesbrough record a 7-4 win.

8TH FEBRUARY 2003

A Geremi free kick – Boro's first away league goal since September – was enough to secure a point at Anfield. The match also witnessed the Middlesbrough debut of John Eustace after he replaced Malcolm Christie with three minutes remaining. The 23-year-old Coventry City loanee was booked soon after coming on in his only notable contribution in a Boro shirt.

9TH FEBRUARY 1985

Having recorded the lowest league attendance in Ayresome Park's history four days earlier, the midweek home fixture with Notts County produced a new record low as only 3,364 witnessed Willie Maddren's men lose 1-0.

9TH FEBRUARY 1988

Boro's FA Cup fourth round tie with Everton was finally decided in the second replay as the First Division champions ran out 2-1 winners at a gusty, rain-swept Goodison Park. The 5,000 travelling Middlesbrough fans were given some cheer after Stuart Ripley equalised in the second half before Tony Mowbray agonisingly turned a Gary Stevens cross into his own net with just seven minutes left on the clock.

10TH FEBRUARY 1973

Marauding left-back Dean Gordon was born in Croydon, London. Starting his professional career at Crystal Palace, Gordon joined Middlesbrough in 1998 after the Teessiders' promotion to the Premier League and the Eagles' relegation to the second tier. In his first season at Middlesbrough he was ever-present and memorably scored a long-range screamer in a famous win at Old Trafford. Injuries blighted his later years at the Riverside and he was released at the end of the 2001/02 season.

11TH FEBRUARY 1911

Boro stopper Tim Williamson returned to the international fold and helped England to a 2-1 win over Ireland in the Home International at Derby County's Baseball Ground.

11TH FEBRUARY 2006

José Mourinho's Chelsea were stunned at the Riverside as Boro outclassed the table-topping Blues with a 3-0 win courtesy of goals from Fábio Rochemback, Stewart Downing and Yakubu.

12TH FEBRUARY 1966

Under pressure from the board and supporters alike and with results showing no sign of improvement, former Mansfield Town and Hull City manager Raich Carter was dismissed as Boro boss with his side lying third from bottom of the Second Division. Trainer Harold Shepherdson stepped up to take over as caretaker manager as Middlesbrough attempted to stave off dropping into the third tier of English football for the first time in the club's history.

13TH **FEBRUARY 1937**

Top scorer Micky Fenton grabbed both goals in Boro's 2-0 win over struggling Liverpool at Anfield to keep the Teessiders in contention for the league championship. The former Portrack Shamrocks striker was unlucky not to grab a hat-trick after having another goal ruled out for offside in what the Football Gazette hailed as the visitors' best performance of the season. The win on Merseyside put the Ayresome Park outfit in sixth place and just four points behind table-topping Charlton Athletic with 13 games remaining. As for Liverpool, the loss left them languishing in 17th spot – just two points clear of the relegation places – and brought the wrath of a jeering crowd as, according to the *Liverpool Echo*, 'Boro simply toyed with them'.

14TH **FEBRUARY 1905**

Middlesbrough smashed the world transfer fee record as they completed the £1,000 signing of Alf Common from Sunderland. It was the second time Common had broken the world record in under a year following his move to Sunderland for £520 in 1904 – a figure surpassed in the same year when Newcastle United signed Andy McCombie from their Wearside rivals. However, neither of the previous two transfers had provoked the level of debate that ensued after Boro paid four figures for their new forward. Press cartoonists depicted Common – labelled with his £1,000 price tag – fighting off the threat of relegation, while a commission appointed by the Football League met in Newcastle the following month to hear evidence in connection to the transfer such was the furore around the lavish expenditure of the Ayresome Park outfit.

14TH **FEBRUARY 1931**

Despite the absence of manager Peter McWilliam from St James' Park, Boro stunned the Magpies in their own backyard with a 5-0 win on Valentine's Day. Freddy Warren opened the scoring in the opening quarter of an hour before Kenny Cameron added a second shortly before half-time. George Camsell scored his customary goal, following in after Billy Pease's strike had hit the bar. Camsell almost doubled his tally but Albert McInroy in the Newcastle goal parried the effort out, only for John McKay to convert Boro's fourth. Camsell was not to be denied his second as he combined with Pease to turn in the former Northampton Town man's cross beyond McInroy.

JOHN McKAY SCORED BORO'S FOURTH IN THE DERBY CLASH (CULLEY COLLECTION)

14TH **FEBRUARY 1988**

Tony Mowbray and Alan Kernaghan were Boro's small-screen heroes as their goals in the last ten minutes helped the team fight back to win 2-1 over Aston Villa in the first Football League match outside of the top flight to be televised live. *The Big Match Live*'s coverage reflected on the club's troubles in recent years before declaring, 'Middlesbrough is once again a football town, and a proud one too.' After the match, studio guest Jack Charlton awarded the man of the match award to Mogga.

14TH **FEBRUARY 2000**

Paul Merson returned to the Riverside Stadium to haunt his former employers as he inspired Aston Villa to a 4-0 win that piled the pressure on Bryan Robson after a run of one point from a possible 15. The Villa side contained not just one former Boro player but also five future ones in George Boateng, Benito Carbone, Ugo Ehiogu, Gareth Southgate and Alan Wright. To make matters worse for the hosts, Paul Gascoigne went off injured with a broken arm after elbowing Boateng.

15TH **FEBRUARY 1997**

Juninho's 77th-minute strike secured a 1-0 win over Manchester City at Maine Road as Boro progressed to the FA Cup quarter-finals for the first time since 1981.

16TH **FEBRUARY 1974**

Boro began a run of nine consecutive wins with a 3-1 victory at Boothferry Park, bringing with it Hull City's first home league defeat of the season. John Hickton's fifth goal of the campaign opened the scoring before David Mills doubled the lead. After the interval Alan Foggon got among the goals, finishing off a through ball from Graeme Souness, before Hull scored a consolation in the dying minutes.

17TH **FEBRUARY 2005**

Two valuable away goals put Boro in control of their two-legged UEFA Cup tie with Graz AK. Boro led twice in Austria through second-half goals from Bolo Zenden and Jimmy Floyd Hasselbaink but each time the hosts fought back.

18TH **FEBRUARY 1876**

According to folklore, it had long been held that Middlesbrough FC was formed at a tripe supper held at the Talbot Hotel on 18th February 1876. However, it is now more widely accepted that the club's origins stemmed from a meeting of the town's cricketers at the gymnasium behind the Albert Park Hotel on Linthorpe Road in October 1876.

18TH FEBRUARY 1995

Having made his debut from the bench in a 1-0 loss to Reading in the previous game, German goal-getter Uwe Fuchs marked his first start for Bryan Robson's men with the only goal of the game as Boro saw off Charlton Athletic in front of 16,301 at Ayresome Park.

18TH FEBRUARY 1998

An already rocking atmosphere at the Riverside Stadium ahead of the League Cup semi-final second leg with Liverpool was turned up to 11 after just two minutes when Paul Merson – who scored in the first leg remembered for Steve Baker's man-marking of Steve McManaman – levelled the tie from the penalty spot after Mikkel Beck was felled in the box by Jamie Carragher. Just two minutes later, debutant Marco Branca ran on to a piercing through ball from former Arsenal man Merson before coolly slotting through PlayStation-loving David James's legs. Despite the Anfield outfit piling on the pressure, Boro held out to secure a record third successive major domestic final appearance.

19TH FEBRUARY 1927

Middlesbrough were well-backed by hundreds of supporters who made the journey south by train to Millwall for an FA Cup fifth round tie complete with a jazz band singing a paraphrase of 'Tipperary' with the words 'It's a long way to go to Wembley … we'll be right there!' Such optimism proved to be misplaced as Millwall raced into a 3-0 lead and Boro suffered a 'tragic tale of two missed penalties', with the normally reliable George Camsell and Billy Pease the culprits. Pease and Owen Williams replied for Boro and the visitors might have had another penalty but ultimately it wasn't to be. Following the disappointing defeat, the Teesside press were able to find some positives, predictably determining 'this dismissal of Middlesbrough from the Cup will free the team's attention for the more important objective … winning back to the First Division'.

19TH FEBRUARY 1997

Boro's League Cup semi-final first leg at Edgeley Park was washed out after a deluge of rain at Stockport County's home ground.

20TH FEBRUARY 1997

Having been linked with Everton and Manchester City, Australian goalkeeper Mark Schwarzer ended a brief spell at Bradford City, managed by Middlesbrough-born Chris Kamara, to make what proved to be an 'unbelievable' £1.25m bargain switch to Boro.

21ST FEBRUARY 1998

A then Riverside Stadium attendance record of 30,227 witnessed Boro gain three precious points in the Tees–Wear derby as Marco Branca grabbed a brace on his league debut. Fellow new signing – and Newcastle United fan – Alun Armstrong enjoyed a dream bow by adding a third goal to announce his arrival from Stockport County in style in the 3-1 win over Sunderland.

22ND FEBRUARY 1902

Boro completed the double over Barnsley as they ran out 7-2 winners at Oakwell. John 'Jack' Brearley scored four of the visitors' goals, with Andrew Davidson, James Leslie and William Wardrobe adding the others.

22ND FEBRUARY 1973

Osvaldo Giroldo Júnior, better known as Juninho, was born in São Paulo, Brazil. Having started his senior career at Ituano – a club he would later return to as player-president – he made his name at São Paulo. Juninho enjoyed a memorable 1995 when he was named Brazilian Footballer of the Year, made his international debut, and scored a free kick against England at Wembley to help his side win the Umbro Cup. After signing for Middlesbrough in October 1995, the star made such an impression that in 1997 – after less than 18 months at the club – he was voted Boro's greatest ever player by fans and second to Graeme Souness by his fellow professionals.

23RD FEBRUARY 1991

Colin Todd's promotion-chasing Boro recorded a vital win over Charlton Athletic at Selhurst Park thanks to a solitary goal from Bernie Slaven. The victory saw Middlesbrough move just one point behind third-placed Sheffield Wednesday.

24TH FEBRUARY 1877

Middlesbrough's first reported match was held against local rugby side Tees Wanderers, although it is thought several games were played before this fixture that have been lost to history. Jackson Ewbank is credited with scoring the club's first reported goal in the 1-1 draw in front of a 'good attendance of visitors'.

24TH FEBRUARY 1996

Bryan Robson's men ended a dismal run of eight consecutive league defeats with a battling draw at Highfield Road. The goalless encounter with Coventry City meant Boro recorded their first point of 1996.

25TH **FEBRUARY 1905**

Middlesbrough goalkeeper Tim Williamson made his England debut at Ayresome Park as Ireland visited Teesside. Unfortunately, the Boro stopper scored an own goal but England managed a draw courtesy of a goal from his future Middlesbrough team-mate Steve Bloomer.

26TH **FEBRUARY 1977**

Want-away star David Mills scored a hat-trick – the club's first in the FA Cup since 1966 – as Boro stunned Arsenal in a 4-1 Ayresome Park win. Boro raced into a two-goal lead with Mills grabbing both. Malcolm Macdonald – better known to younger readers as one of the Three Legends that dominated the football talkshow airwaves of the north-east in the 1990s and 2000s – pulled a goal back for Arsenal in the 27th minute. Boro pushed on after the break and David Armstrong restored the two-goal lead before both teams hit the bar. With time almost up, Mills scored his third and Boro's fourth as he slid home a rebound from Terry Cooper's saved effort.

26TH **FEBRUARY 1997**

The rearranged League Cup semi-final first leg against Stockport County saw Boro come away from Edgeley Park with a 2-0 victory as they edged close to a first major Wembley final. New signing Mark Schwarzer made his debut and impressed between the sticks with a commanding performance. Despite dominating play, it was not until the 73rd minute that the visitors broke the deadlock as Mikkel Beck beat the offside trap and slid the ball beyond Paul Jones in the home side's goal. Six minutes later, Fabrizio Ravanelli scored after Jones could only parry Craig Hignett's effort and the Italian hammered home with his second attempt after his first shot was cleared off the line.

27TH **FEBRUARY 1937**

Boro recovered from the disappointment of derby defeat to Sunderland in their last outing to hammer Huddersfield 5-0 in their biggest win of the season. Incredibly, all of the game's goals came in the first half as the Teessiders went level on points with third-placed Manchester City in the First Division.

28TH **FEBRUARY 1903**

Middlesbrough lost for the last time at their Linthorpe Road Ground as Liverpool headed back to Merseyside with a 2-0 win.

29TH FEBRUARY 2004

After 128 years of waiting, Middlesbrough finally won a major trophy. A crowd of 72,634 packed into Cardiff's Millennium Stadium and witnessed a frantic opening to the League Cup Final as Boro raced into a two-goal lead over Bolton Wanderers in the opening seven minutes. Gaizka Mendieta's cross-field pass set Bolo Zenden running down the left and the Dutchman crossed low for Joseph-Désiré Job to slide in at the back post to put Middlesbrough into a second-minute lead and record the then fastest goal in a League Cup Final. The Trotters almost replied immediately through World Cup winner Youri Djorkaeff but Mark Schwarzer saved at his near post. Boro responded and as Job burst into the box, former Sunderland defender Emerson Thome tripped the Cameroon international and referee Mike Riley awarded a penalty. Zenden stepped up to take the spot kick and slipped as he made contact with the ball – replays showed that he touched the ball twice – but nevertheless his effort found its way past Jussi Jääskeläinen. Boro were 2-0 up after seven minutes and appeared to be cruising until Schwarzer allowed Kevin Davies's weak shot to creep in at his near post. Despite the error, the Australian stopper redeemed himself with several notable saves, including a double stop from Per Frandsen and Djorkaeff. The second half brought fewer clear-cut chances, and one notable incident came when Ugo Ehiogu appeared to handle a Stelios shot in the box but appeals for a penalty were turned down. In the dying seconds, Boro broke with Juninho running from his own half but as he raced towards goal he was thwarted by Bruno N'Gotty. It proved to be the last touch of the game by a Boro player and seconds later after Jääskeläinen desperately launched the ball forward, Riley blew the final whistle, prompting wild scenes in the Middlesbrough end as Juninho sunk to the floor in celebration. It was then left to captain Gareth Southgate to hold the trophy aloft and signal the end of Boro's cup hoodoo. Steve Gibson celebrated with the players on the pitch, Sam Allardyce used his post-match interview to bemoan Bolton missing out on a penalty, and Juninho ranked winning the trophy as an achievement that paralleled winning the World Cup. Boro's League Cup-winning line-up was: Mark Schwarzer, Danny Mills, Frank Queudrue, Ugo Ehiogu, Gareth Southgate, George Boateng, Doriva, Gaizka Mendieta, Juninho, Joseph-Désiré Job (Michael Ricketts 65), Bolo Zenden. The unused substitutes were: Brad Jones, Chris Riggott, Stewart Downing, Massimo Maccarone.

DORIVA AND JUNINHO ARE ALL SMILES AFTER WINNING THE LEAGUE CUP IN CARDIFF (THE GAZETTE)

MIDDLESBROUGH
On This Day

MARCH

1ST MARCH 2022

Nineteen-year-old Josh Coburn fired Championship side Middlesbrough into the FA Cup quarter-finals at a sold-out Riverside Stadium. The youngster's 107th-minute strike was enough to down Antonio Conte's Tottenham Hotspur, with the 1-0 win giving Chris Wilder's rejuvenated team their eighth successive home win.

2ND MARCH 1901

Scottish inside-forward John Wilkie scored five times in a 9-2 trouncing of Gainsborough Trinity at the Linthorpe Road Ground in the third of a five-game winning run for the Teessiders.

2ND MARCH 1974

Boro recorded a 2-0 win at Roker Park in an incident-packed match to complete a double over Sunderland. Goals from David Mills and Alan Foggon put the Mackems to the stake; they also had Bobby Kerr and Dennis Tueart sent off to add to their woes.

3RD MARCH 1906

Struggling at the wrong end of the First Division table, Middlesbrough upset the odds and claimed a vital two points with a derby win over the previous season's champions, Newcastle United, at Ayresome Park. A crowd of 20,000 turned out for the game billed as the 'battle of the North' in the local press, with Robert Henry Walker's second-half strike separating the sides.

4TH MARCH 1992

The visit of Manchester United for the League Cup semi-final first leg brought a sell-out crowd at Ayresome Park. Boro put the Red Devils under pressure in the first half and Gary Parkinson's long-range drive was kept out by a great save from Peter Schmeichel, before the great Dane then blocked Bernie Slaven at close range. Into the second half, future Boro captain Paul Ince's header was saved by Stephen Pears in a fine display by the former Old Trafford stopper that prompted chants of 'England's number one'.

4TH MARCH 1995

The Holgate had a new goalscoring hero in the form of on-loan German Uwe Fuchs after the Kaiserslautern forward scored a hat-trick to give Boro a 3-0 win over Bristol City. After Fuchs opened the scoring in the first half, the Robins were then reduced to ten men following Wayne Allison's dismissal for a rash tackle on Steve Vickers. Fuchs added two further clinical strikes in the second half to cement the home team's victory.

DAVID MILLS WAS ON THE SCORESHEET AS BORO RAN OUT 2-0 WINNERS AT ROKER PARK.

4TH MARCH 1998

In the second match of his second spell at the club, Andy Dibble endured a horror show at Loftus Road as he conceded five goals in a hammering by QPR. The shock defeat made it nine goals conceded in two matches by the former Manchester City and Wales goalkeeper after he had leaked four in a weekend loss to promotion rivals Nottingham Forest at the City Ground.

5TH MARCH 2003

Over three weeks after the controversial postponement of Boro's home league clash with north-east rivals Newcastle United, the Teessiders stunned the title-chasing Magpies as Geremi's goal delivered the visitors' first defeat in two months in front of a ground-record 34,814 spectators at the Riverside.

6TH MARCH 1976

Middlesbrough stunned Bob Paisley's Liverpool with a well-deserved 2-0 win at Anfield. The Kop was silenced as Terry Cooper put Boro into the lead after just two minutes and their despair was compounded when John Hickton added the visitors' second after 28 minutes. The result was Liverpool's last defeat of the season as they went on to win both the First Division and the UEFA Cup.

7TH MARCH 1960

Gordon Jones signed professional forms for Middlesbrough. Defender Jones would go on to make more post-war and outfield appearances for Boro than any other player with 527 appearances (457 league), a total bettered only by goalkeeper Tim Williamson's 602 (563 league).

8TH MARCH 2009

Having led at half-time through a David Wheater header at Goodison Park, Boro crashed out of the FA Cup at the quarter-final stage after Everton staged a comeback through goals from Marouane Fellaini and Louis Saha.

9TH MARCH 1930

Presiding at the annual Sportsmen Service of the Middlesbrough Brotherhood, Boro director and mayor of Redcar Alderman W. Metcalf condemned barracking by Middlesbrough supporters, claiming one particular section of the Ayresome Park crowd attended only to abuse players. Revealing he had heard some barrackers state at the end of matches that they would never attend again, he told the gathering how he wished they would keep away. Metcalf considered gambling to be the main cause of the abuse and encouraged the public not to lead players into temptation.

ALDERMAN METCALFE WAS CRITICAL OF THE BEHAVIOUR OF SOME OF THE CLUB'S FANS (CULLEY COLLECTION)

9TH MARCH 1938

A sensational 6-1 win at Manchester City proved to be a memorable day for Tom Cochrane, who set Boro on the way to victory within a minute – with some sources suggesting the goal was scored after a record six seconds – when indecision in the Maine Road defence saw Billy Brown's sliced shot across the box finished off by the former Leeds United man. The goal was Cochrane's first of his four in the game, while Micky Fenton bagged a brace.

9TH MARCH 2006

Yakubu converted a 12th-minute penalty, awarded after Jimmy Floyd Hasselbaink was felled by Italian under-21 goalkeeper Gianluca Curci, to grab the all-important goal that separated Boro and Roma at the Riverside in the UEFA Cup last-16 clash. The Nigerian's winner came after a hectic start in which Ashton-under-Lyne-born Azzurri international Simone Perotta managed to steer the ball beyond Mark Schwarzer in the home goal but not beyond the retreating Gareth Southgate, who made a last-ditch clearance. A resolute defensive performance from Steve McClaren's side with Southgate and George Boateng outstanding ensured the Teessiders took a goal advantage to the Olympic Stadium.

9TH MARCH 2008

Live on the BBC, second-tier Cardiff City stunned Boro at the Riverside Stadium as the Premier League outfit turned in an abysmal performance in the FA Cup quarter-final. The result meant eventual winners Portsmouth were the only Premier League representatives in the semi-finals as Middlesbrough faltered when in arguably the strongest position they had ever been in to lift the trophy.

10TH MARCH 2005

After having a penalty appeal turned down in the opening minute, Boro were cast aside by Sporting Lisbon as the visitors raced into a three-goal lead that left the Riverside shell-shocked and seemingly ended all hopes of progressing to the UEFA Cup quarter-finals. However, Boro rallied with two late goals – a spectacular overhead kick by Joseph-Désiré Job and a close-range effort from Chris Riggott – that kept the tie alive ahead of the second leg at the Estádio José Alvalade the following week.

11TH MARCH 1933

Micky Fenton signed professional forms for Middlesbrough, who made a donation of £10 to his former club South Bank East End. The Stockton-on-Tees striker bagged 147 league goals and an official total of 162 goals for Boro – becoming the club's fifth-highest all-time scorer – and also served as trainer and reserve team coach during his 32-year stay.

11TH **MARCH 1992**

Boro suffered heartbreak at Old Trafford in the second leg of the League Cup semi-final with Manchester United. After falling behind to a Lee Sharpe goal in the first half, Lennie Lawrence's side fought back and Bernie Slaven grabbed a well-deserved equaliser five minutes into the second period. The course of Middlesbrough FC history might well have been very different had former Boro man Gary Pallister not managed to get back to clear John Hendrie's goal-bound effort off the line as the gates of Wembley were opening wide for the Teessiders. Into extra time, Boro continued to toil and Willie Falconer was denied by Peter Schmeichel before Ryan Giggs's goal crushed the visitors' dreams of a visit to Wembley.

11TH **MARCH 1998**

After two successive defeats in which they had conceded nine goals without reply, Boro faced Swindon Town at the Riverside knowing that six goals and a win would return them to the top of the First Division. A brace each from Alun Armstrong, Marco Branca and Neil Maddison – with the Italian scoring a late overhead kick to complete a 6-0 rout – ensured Boro got back to winning ways in the most spectacular of manners.

12TH **MARCH 1997**

A 1-0 home defeat to Stockport County is an unlikely celebratory occasion in a club's history but for Middlesbrough the result meant that they would appear in their first major Wembley cup final. Sean Connolly scored after just five minutes to net his first goal for Stockport, but the home side held on after the shock and stumbled their way to the League Cup Final with a 2-1 aggregate win.

13TH **MARCH 1899**

As Boro pushed to raise funds to become a professional outfit, at a meeting of the club's directors it was reported that promises to take up 800 shares had been received and Lincoln City officials had provided assurances that they would support Middlesbrough's application for admission to the Second Division of the Football League.

14TH MARCH 1898

At a meeting of the Cleveland Association, Boro found themselves at odds with authorities and forthcoming opponents South Bank as debates raged over whether a Cleveland Senior Cup semi-final scheduled for the following Saturday should go ahead given the smallpox epidemic in Middlesbrough. Eston Urban District Council demanded the tie's postponement but Boro refused, pointing to the crowds from South Bank and Middlesbrough that frequently mixed at the Saturday markets. The Cleveland Association chairman considered it 'the height of folly to bring a crowd together to stand one and a half to two hours for there would be a great danger of the infection spreading' but the meeting voted six to two in favour of the match going ahead.

14TH MARCH 1978

Following a stalemate with Second Division Leyton Orient at Ayresome Park with Billy Ashcroft guilty of a bad miss from six yards out, Boro knew a win at Brisbane Road in the FA Cup quarter-final replay would see them progress to their first semi-final appearance and a clash with Arsenal – the club they had knocked out of the tournament the previous season. However, the O's stunned their top-flight visitors courtesy of two early long-range efforts from Peter Kitchen and Joe Mayo. David Armstrong pulled a goal back with five minutes remaining but Orient held on to progress to their first FA Cup semi-final.

15TH MARCH 1975

Scottish midfielder Graeme Souness returned to haunt his former club as he scored a brace in a 3-0 win over struggling Tottenham Hotspur at Ayresome Park. John Hickton scored Boro's other goal.

15TH MARCH 2006

Middlesbrough produced a stunning performance in Rome as they knocked Roma out of the UEFA Cup on away goals following a 2-1 loss in the Italian capital. Leading 1-0 from the first leg, Jimmy Floyd Hasselbaink doubled Boro's aggregate lead after 32 minutes with a powerful header. The Italians equalled the score on the night through a Mancini goal just before half-time, with the Brazilian then adding a second for the home side from the spot after 66 minutes following an onslaught on the Boro goal. A tense finale threatened to boil over as players from each team squared up to each other and in the final minute Philippe Mexès was dismissed after picking up a second yellow card following a bad foul on Stewart Downing. Boro held on to record one of the most memorable results in their history.

16TH MARCH 1996

Boro gained their first home point of the year courtesy of a Robbie Mustoe equaliser just a minute after on-loan Oxford United man Chris Allen had given Nottingham Forest – with one eye on a UEFA Cup quarter-final with Bayern Munich three days later – a second-half lead.

17TH MARCH 1995

Bryan Robson dismissed transfer speculation linking Boro with a £1m bid for Norwich City's promising teenage striker Jamie Cureton.

18TH MARCH 1995

Irish defender Keith O'Halloran made a debut to forget as Derby County stunned Bryan Robson's promotion-chasing side, powering to a 3-0 half-time lead at Ayresome Park. The full-back was hauled off at the break and although Boro staged a fightback after the break through goals from Uwe Fuchs and Jamie Pollock, the Rams added another goal to hand the hosts their biggest home defeat of the season.

19TH MARCH 1974

Boro triumphed 4-0 on the road for the second time in three days as centre-half pairing Willie Maddren (two) and Stuart Boam were unlikely goal-getters on Bobby Moore's debut for Fulham. Leading through Maddren's first-half diving header, Boro had to wait until the 75th minute for Graeme Souness to extend their lead. Maddren added his second goal in the 80th minute before captain Boam completed the scoring with only a few minutes remaining. The victory put Boro 11 points clear at the Second Division summit.

20TH MARCH 1998

The Scotsman reported that Paul Gascoigne was poised to depart Rangers and join former England team-mate Bryan Robson on Teesside, suggesting the friendship between the two made Boro favourites to secure Gazza's signature ahead of fellow suitors Crystal Palace.

21ST MARCH 1995

A rainy Roker Park failed to dampen Boro's promotion charge as a bundled second-half goal from Jamie Pollock proved enough to give Bryan Robson's men the points in a tempestuous derby that saw fighting break out on the pitch between fans and stewards and Sunderland supporters turn on manager Mick Buxton. The three points saw the Teessiders leapfrog Tranmere Rovers to go one point clear at the top of the First Division with nine games remaining.

22ND MARCH 1969

Boro leapfrogged Cardiff City to move into second place in the Second Division following a 5-3 win over Hull City at Ayresome Park. John Hickton was the hero as he scored four goals, with Eric McMordie adding the home side's other strike in the victory that moved the Teessiders just four points behind Brian Clough's Derby County.

23RD MARCH 1974

Boro secured promotion as David Armstrong scored the only goal against Oxford United. Orient's 1-0 loss at Hillsborough left the Londoners trailing Boro by an unassailable 17 points and with it ensured Jack Charlton's side returned to the top flight in his first season in management – and with eight games to spare.

23RD MARCH 1995

Boro set a club transfer record and underlined their ambitions with the £1.3m signing of 25-goal Norwegian international Jan Åge Fjørtoft from Swindon Town. Bryan Robson had initially enquired about the First Division's top scorer two months earlier but was rebuffed by the Wiltshire club who were then League Cup semi-finalists and still in the FA Cup. While the USA '94 World Cup star's transfer excited fans on Teesside, the switch prompted fury among the Swindon faithful as the club lost their prized asset and subsequently suffered their second consecutive relegation. On the same day, Phil Whelan signed on at Ayresome Park following a £300,000 switch from Ipswich Town but the FA did not receive the relevant paperwork in time to allow the former England under-21 man to play for Middlesbrough during the remainder of the season.

24TH MARCH 1988

Bruce Rioch snapped up unsettled Watford striker Trevor Senior in a £200,000 deal – one of the largest fees of transfer deadline day – as he looked to add firepower to Boro's promotion push.

25TH MARCH 1990

Boro made their first appearance at Wembley as they faced Chelsea in the Zenith Data Systems Cup Final. More than 35,000 Boro fans made the journey to London for the historic occasion. Although missing out through injury, Tony Mowbray was afforded the honour of leading the side out. The match proved to be a scrappy encounter of few clear-cut chances. Bernie Slaven looked set to give Middlesbrough an early lead but he was denied by a last-ditch interception by Chelsea's Peter Nicholas, who took the ball off the striker's toes. Midway through the first half, Stephen Pears got a hand to a Tony Dorigo free kick but could not keep it out and the former Aston Villa man's strike proved to be the only goal of the game. The historic Boro line-up was: Stephen Pears, Gary Parkinson, Colin Cooper, Alan Kernaghan, Simon Coleman, Owen McGee, Stuart Ripley, Mark Proctor, Mark Brennan, Bernie Slaven, Peter Davenport.

26TH MARCH 1995

Bryan Robson scored his only competitive goal for Middlesbrough with a long-range strike after 14 minutes to set his side on the way to a home win over Port Vale live on Tyne Tees Television. New signing Jan Åge Fjørtoft missed out due to international commitments with Norway but Boro managed without their £1.3m man as further goals from Steve Vickers and Uwe Fuchs helped them to a 3-0 victory that moved them four points clear of second-placed Bolton Wanderers.

27TH MARCH 1936

Champions-elect Sunderland were stunned at Ayresome Park as Middlesbrough turned on the style to hammer the Wearsiders 6-0 – their heaviest defeat of the campaign and Boro's first win over their rivals since October 1930. With the Mackems trailing 5-0, future Boro manager Raich Carter was dismissed after allegedly kicking out at right-back Billy Brown, before the visitors were reduced to nine men after Bert Davis was dismissed for dissent.

28TH MARCH 1990

Scottish goalscorer Bernie Slaven made his debut for the Republic of Ireland and announced his arrival on the international scene with the only goal of the game against an injury-hit Wales in a pre-Italia '90 friendly at Lansdowne Road. The Boro frontman scored with only five minutes remaining, reacting first after Kevin Sheedy's penalty was saved by his Everton team-mate Neville Southall.

29TH MARCH 1998

Middlesbrough appeared in a record third successive domestic cup final as they contested the League Cup with Chelsea, the side who had beaten them ten months earlier in the FA Cup Final. There was no place for new signing Paul Gascoigne in the Wembley starting line-up, with the former Rangers man having to instead settle for a place on the bench. In the 65th minute, Bryan Robson attempted to introduce some creativity to a scrappy game as he replaced the ineffective Hámilton Ricard with Gascoigne. It meant Gazza was making his Boro debut at the stadium where he had played his last domestic game in English football, the 1991 FA Cup Final, when he was stretchered off with torn cruciate ligaments after a terrible challenge on Nottingham Forest's Gary Charles. There was, however, to be no redemption story for either Gazza or Middlesbrough as the Teessiders suffered Wembley heartbreak at the hands of Chelsea for the third time through extra-time goals from Frank Sinclair and Roberto Di Matteo. After the match, Gazza gave his runners-up medal to Craig Hignett – the man whose place he had taken on the bench – in a heartfelt gesture towards his new team-mate.

30TH MARCH 2006

Boro suffered a 2-0 defeat to FC Basel in the first leg of their UEFA Cup quarter-final in Switzerland. Basel took the lead after 43 minutes when Matías Delgado's long-range effort beat Mark Schwarzer after a wicked bounce. Just two minutes later the home side doubled their lead through midfielder David Degen, leaving Middlesbrough – without an away goal – with a huge deficit to make up in the second leg.

31ST MARCH 2004

Boro captain Gareth Southgate played 45 minutes as a second-half substitute as England suffered a 1-0 friendly loss, Zlatan Ibrahimović's goal extending the Three Lions' 36-year winless streak against Sweden.

MIDDLESBROUGH
On This Day

APRIL

1st APRIL 1995

Assistant manager Viv Anderson created history when he became Middlesbrough's oldest ever debutant at the age of 38 years, eight months and three days old as he stepped in for the suspended Nigel Pearson at the heart of defence. He was joined in making his bow at The Hawthorns by new signing Jan Åge Fjørtoft. Trailing 1-0 at half-time, an Alan Moore-inspired comeback ensured it was a memorable occasion for the new additions to the line-up. The diminutive Irishman set up Jamie Pollock for the equaliser before Paul Raven turned a Moore cross into his own net. The youngster topped off a fine second-half performance by getting on the scoresheet himself to give the visitors a 3-1 win.

2nd APRIL 1898

Middlesbrough's FA Amateur Cup semi-final against Thornaby was played in secret at Brotton after a smallpox epidemic in the 'Ironopolis' brought chaos to the club's hunt for glory. Initially scheduled to take place in Darlington, local officials refused to allow the match to go ahead in the railway town for fear of the unwelcome arrival of smallpox. Boro's directors refused to embrace the FA's suggestion that they should pull out of the tie and eventually it was decided that the game should be played 'with closed gates' and 'only players be allowed to take part who have medical certificates as to their freedom from the disease'. Catherine Budd's Sport in Urban England confirmed the secretive nature of the tie's venue, citing a contemporary report that stated though 'many keen footballists had been on the alert for the past few days, those who knew the location of the match were very limited in number'. The drama ahead of the tie was matched by the action in East Cleveland as Boro fought back from a goal down to reach the final courtesy of goals from Bishop and Wanless.

2nd APRIL 1988

Boro smashed Sheffield United for six at Ayresome Park with Stuart Ripley and new boy Trevor Senior stars of the show. It was Senior – in only his second Middlesbrough appearance – who opened the scoring before Ripley doubled the home side's lead after rounding the goalkeeper and firing the ball into an empty net. A minute before the interval, Rippers beat the offside trap and chipped the on-rushing goalkeeper to make it 3-0 at half-time. Three minutes after the restart, Bernie Slaven added the fourth before Ripley completed the first senior hat-trick of his Boro career. The win saw Boro leapfrog Blackburn Rovers into second place in the Second Division – just two points behind leaders Aston Villa with a game in hand.

3rd APRIL 1915

Chaos ensued at wartime Ayresome Park as Boro's match against Oldham Athletic was abandoned after Latics defender Bill Cook refused to leave the field after being sent off. The incident occurred after referee Mr H. Smith had not only failed to award the visitors a penalty after which Boro broke away to score a third goal, but then awarded a penalty against Cook after he felled Jackie Carr. It was all too much for Cook, who lashed out at the South Bank lad – who historian Harry Glasper described as having 'won his club many penalties by verbally goading an opposition defender' – and was dismissed. The best efforts of other players to encourage Cook to depart failed and the referee walked off the pitch and was followed by the two sides. Ultimately, the charismatic Latics stopper – also among several footballers from the era to play first-class cricket – was hauled before the Football Commission at Manchester and handed a lengthy ban and ordered to pay the costs of the hearing, where it was also determined that the 4-1 scoreline should stand.

3rd APRIL 1946

Alf Common, the world's first £1,000 footballer when he signed for Boro in 1905, died in hospital at Darlington aged 65.

3rd APRIL 1972

Youngster David Armstrong made his Boro debut, aged just 17 years and 98 days, in a 3-1 loss at Blackpool.

3rd APRIL 1982

The 100th league meeting between Middlesbrough and Sunderland attracted a crowd of just 19,006 – the lowest for a Tees–Wear derby at Roker Park since the Second World War – and witnessed bottom-place Boro leapfrog the Rokerites on goal difference as both sides battled to avoid the dreaded drop to the second tier. Former Sunderland full-back Joe Bolton returned to Roker as the only change from the league draw at home to Manchester City a week earlier. Boro broke the deadlock in the 34th minute when David Hodgson beat two men and crossed for the on-rushing Billy Ashcroft to get the slightest of touches to direct the ball into the net. Sunderland had chances to draw level but it was Boro who broke away to score the game's second goal in the 78th minute as centre-half Mick Baxter hammered the ball into the back of Sunderland's net then ran to celebrate with the fans in the away end.

4TH APRIL 1964

Cláudio Ibrahim Vaz Leal, better known as Branco, was born in Bagé, Brazil. A World Cup winner in 1994, two years later the 30-year-old free agent joined fellow Brazilian international Juninho at the Riverside in a high-profile move.

5TH APRIL 1996

Andy Campbell, aged just 16 years and 352 days, became the club's youngest Premier League debutant when he came off the bench in an impressive 3-1 Good Friday win over Sheffield Wednesday that all-but sealed their top-flight survival. A brace from Jan Åge Fjørtoft and a Premier League debut goal from former Arnold Town striker Chris Freestone were enough to seal the points despite Mark Pembridge's impressive equaliser for the Owls.

6TH APRIL 1997

Middlesbrough made their first appearance at a major Wembley cup final in a clash with fellow top-flight outfit Leicester City. Some 35,000 Boro fans made the trip to the Twin Towers for the League Cup Final and were in confident mood ahead of the tie, with a Juninho-inspired team having humbled the Foxes in a 3-1 win at Filbert Street just weeks earlier. After a goalless 90 minutes in which Boro had enjoyed the better chances and both sides hit the woodwork through Emile Heskey and Fabrizio Ravanelli, Boro finally made the breakthrough five minutes into extra time. Having been well-marshalled by Pontus Kåmark, Juninho broke free from the Swede's shackles and burst into the Leicester penalty area and – with Neil Lennon unable to fully clear the ball – Boro's grey-haired Italian lashed the ball home from close range for the club's first Wembley goal. Yet heartbreak was on the horizon with the Teessiders within touching distance of the trophy when Heskey capitalised from a goalmouth scramble with just two minutes remaining to take the match to a replay at Hillsborough. The historic Boro line-up was: Mark Schwarzer, Neil Cox, Curtis Fleming, Nigel Pearson, Gianluca Festa, Craig Hignett, Robbie Mustoe, Emerson, Juninho, Fabrizio Ravanelli, Mikkel Beck. Subs: Steve Vickers, Clayton Blackmore, Alan Moore.

6TH APRIL 2006

Boro staged a stunning UEFA Cup quarter-final comeback against FC Basel to reach the semi-finals in only the club's second season in Europe. Leading 2-0 from the first leg, the Swiss side made it 3-0 on aggregate after 23 minutes. What followed was then arguably the greatest comeback in European football history with Mark Viduka scoring on 33 minutes to level the score on the night. Into the second half, the Australian international grabbed another before Jimmy Floyd Hasselbaink levelled the aggregate scores – although with Basel still ahead on away goals. With the clock ticking and time almost up, it was Massimo Maccarone who proved to be the hero of the hour. With two minutes remaining, the substitute squeezed the ball home from a narrow angle after Pascal Zuberbühler could only parry a Fábio Rochemback long-range effort into the path of the Italian. The goal led commentator Ali Brownlee to acclaim 'the greatest comeback since Lazarus' before declaring at full time, 'The Swiss have rolled. William Tell, it doesn't matter, Heidi, the lot of you, you've taken a pasting at the Riverside … this has been the most magnificent of comebacks, the greatest night the Riverside has ever, ever seen.'

7TH APRIL 1958

Brian Clough strengthened his claims for an England call-up as he scored a hat-trick in a 5-1 home win over Grimsby Town. Welsh star Bill Harris and youngster Alan Peacock added the home side's other goals.

8TH APRIL 1961

After a 6-1 triumph over the Teessiders at Kenilworth Road earlier in the season, Luton Town were on the end of a Brian Clough-inspired loss at Ayresome Park as the Grove Hill goal-getter scored a brace for a patched-up home side in a 2-1 victory.

9TH APRIL 1988

Goals from Stuart Ripley and Gary Hamilton put Bruce Rioch's team in a great position for a second successive promotion as they saw off Manchester City in front of a crowd of 19,443 at Ayresome Park. With Aston Villa only drawing at Selhurst Park after Ian Wright had equalised late on after David Platt had given Villa the lead, Boro's win left them second and just one point behind leaders Millwall with four games remaining.

10TH APRIL 1928

Willie Millar, Billy Pease, debutant Allan Hall and Bobbie Bruce all got on the scoresheet as Boro left Leeds Road with a stunning 4-2 win over top-of-the-table Huddersfield Town. The result was all the more impressive given that the visitors had trailed 2-0 at the interval and had hardly been in the game. The astonishing comeback proved to be not only arguably Middlesbrough's best win of the campaign but also their last.

11TH APRIL 1903

Blackburn Rovers were hammered 4-0 in front of a crowd of 10,000 at the Linthorpe Road Ground. Boro's win, combined with Grimsby Town's loss at title-chasing Sheffield United, ensured the club's new Ayresome Park home would be playing host to top-flight football in its maiden campaign.

12TH APRIL 2016

A 94th-minute goal from substitute Adam Forshaw propelled Boro to the top of the Championship in dramatic fashion. With Middlesbrough in front through an Emilio Nsue first-half goal, Simon Cox's effort drew Reading level. However, following a pinball-like scramble in the dying seconds, the former Everton man kept his composure to tuck the ball home.

13TH APRIL 1895

Middlesbrough reached their first national final after a 4-0 win over the Lancaster Regiment in the FA Amateur Cup semi-final in front of fewer than 1,000 at Derby. One story from the match is that only a solitary Middlesbrough fan made the trip to support the team!

13TH APRIL 1936

George Camsell bagged four goals and fellow England international Ralph Birkett the other as Boro hammered Sheffield Wednesday 5-0 at Ayresome Park in the side's last win of the season.

13TH APRIL 1997

Boro headed to Old Trafford as red-hot favourites in their first FA Cup semi-final, with third-tier Chesterfield standing between them and a place in the final. However, with the game goalless, the match turned on its head after the Teessiders' Slovakian full-back Vladimír Kinder was dismissed late in the first half after picking up a second yellow card in a tussle with Kevin Davies. Into the second half and with the Spireites spurred on by their numerical advantage, the Saltergate side took the lead courtesy of a close-range finish by Andy Morris after Ben Roberts could only parry Davies's effort into the forward's path. Ten-men Boro's dreams of a first FA Cup Final appearance seemed all but over when Sean Dyche doubled the underdogs' lead from the penalty spot. Boro rallied and pulled a goal back courtesy of a close-range Ravanelli strike before Juninho was felled by Dyche and Craig Hignett squeezed the subsequent penalty past Billy Mercer in the Chesterfield goal. Into extra time, Gianluca Festa hammered the Teessiders into the lead after a frantic assault on the Chesterfield goal, before – for the second time in a week – Boro experienced late heartache as Jamie Hewitt, the man from Chesterfield, headed past a hapless Roberts to set up a replay at Hillsborough.

14TH APRIL 1958

Despite Boro's insistence that their star striker was not for sale, Brian Clough continued to be linked with a move away from Ayresome Park. The most recent speculation suggested Everton had tabled a rejected £30,000 bid for the Grove Hill goal ace.

14TH APRIL 2001

Terry Venables' Boro won the Premier League – for Manchester United – with a rip-roaring display at Arsenal. Few had given struggling Boro hope heading to north London but own goals from the Gunners' Brazilian pair Edu and Sylvinho handed the visitors an unlikely 2-0 half-time lead. To hammer home that Middlesbrough's supremacy was no fluke, 'Ham the Man' Ricard added a third after the break and Boro could have had more in one of the biggest shock results in Premier League history and Middlesbrough's first win at Highbury since 1939.

15TH APRIL 1995

A late equaliser from German substitute Uwe Fuchs at bottom side Notts County rescued a point for table-topping Boro after an upset looked on the cards following Devon White's opener.

16TH APRIL 1983

Boro secured their first away win of 1983 courtesy of a 3-0 victory at Blundell Park, moving Malcolm Allison's side up from second-bottom to 16th place. Paul Sugrue set the goals flowing just before the interval after beating three men before curling the ball past the Mariners' goalkeeper. On 52 minutes, Scottish schemer Gary Hamilton scored his first Boro goal to double the lead and with four minutes remaining, Dutch star Heine Otto tapped home a third for the visitors.

16TH APRIL 1997

A dismal League Cup Final replay at Sheffield Wednesday's Hillsborough – the last to be decided by a second match – was settled by a solitary goal by Steve Claridge in extra time to end Boro's hopes of winning the trophy for another year.

17TH APRIL 1976

The *Sunday Mirror* raved that Jack Charlton's search for a new goalscorer might have been solved in his own backyard after defender Tony McAndrew, 20 years and six days of age, took his chance playing up front as he became the youngest Boro player to score a top-flight hat-trick in his side's 3-0 triumph over Sheffield United at Ayresome Park.

18TH APRIL 1949

An Alex McCrae goal and two George Hardwick second-half penalties boosted Boro's First Division survival chances as they recorded a 3-2 win over Newcastle United in front of 44,037 at Ayresome Park. Defeat left the Magpies' title dreams in tatters as they trailed Portsmouth by four points with the Fratton Park outfit also having a game in hand.

19TH APRIL 1975

Boro went out on a high in their final home match of their first season back in the top flight as title-chasing Liverpool were undone by a solitary Alan Foggon goal after 38 minutes in an entertaining game. In his post-match interview Bob Paisley declared the contest could have ended 6-5 to Boro, such was the number of chances created and missed by both sides. The standing ovation afforded to both sets of players after the final whistle provided scant consolation for the Scousers with the result ending their title challenge as Dave Mackay's Derby County claimed the First Division title.

19TH APRIL 1977

John Hickton celebrated a much-deserved testimonial by scoring a hat-trick as Boro hammered arch-rivals Sunderland 6-1 at Ayresome Park.

JOHN HICKTON
TESTIMONIAL MATCH

AYRESOME PARK TUESDAY 19th APRIL 1977

MIDDLESBROUGH v SUNDERLAND

Programme 10p

BORO PAID TRIBUTE TO JOHN HICKTON WITH A TESTIMONIAL MATCH AT AYRESOME PARK AGAINST SUNDERLAND (MIDDLESBROUGH FC)

19TH APRIL 1997

Boro suffered a devastating 1-0 defeat to fellow strugglers and local rivals Sunderland to leave themselves in major relegation trouble. To make matters worse for the home side, the killer blow was delivered by Middlesbrough-born Darren Williams, who celebrated in front of the Boro fans after scoring his team's goal. Despite Williams's jubilation, the goal was ultimately in vain as Sunderland were relegated along with Boro. The Teessiders made an immediate return to the top flight the following season, while Sunderland – with Williams in defence – conceded four goals in a dramatic 4-4 draw play-off final that the Wearsiders lost on penalties to Charlton Athletic.

19TH APRIL 2004

Having lost out in the two-legged final against Manchester United the previous year, Middlesbrough's youth team followed in the footsteps of the League Cup-winning first team by adding further silverware to the Riverside trophy cabinet as they won the club's first FA Youth Cup. Having won 3-0 at Aston Villa in the first leg, Mark Proctor's side finished the job at the Riverside with a 1-0 win.

20TH APRIL 1974

After the Second Division championship trophy was paraded before the match, Boro recorded their biggest home win since 1958 as they steamrolled Sheffield Wednesday. Former Hillsborough man John Hickton opened the scoring, followed by David Mills and Bobby Murdoch goals before the break. Graeme Souness grabbed a brace to make it 5-0, before Alan Foggon added number six and Souness scored again to complete his only Boro hat-trick. Foggon added a goal late on to give Jack Charlton's men an 8-0 victory.

21ST APRIL 1973

Boro's penultimate home fixture of the season saw potential new boss and England World Cup winner Jack Charlton in the Ayresome Park directors' box as he ran the rule over the side as they triumphed 3-0 over Sheffield Wednesday.

JOHN CRAGGS, WILLIE MADDREN AND FRANK SPRAGGON HOLD THE DIVISION 2 TROPHY ALOFT AT AYRESOME PARK (THE GAZETTE)

22ND APRIL 1977

Jack Charlton departed his role as manager of Middlesbrough after just under four years in charge at Ayresome Park. Long linked with a move away from Teesside, including to the burgeoning soccer scene in the United States, Charlton made the announcement as his side prepared for their forthcoming visit to Ipswich Town. The former Leeds United man told the press, 'I have nothing in mind for the immediate future. This is not a hurried decision. It was time I had a change.'

22ND APRIL 1995

In a match remembered for a torrential downpour at Oakwell, Jan Åge Fjørtoft scored his second goal in two matches as Bryan Robson's men left Barnsley with a point.

23RD APRIL 1898

Having played on through a smallpox epidemic in Middlesbrough that threatened to derail the club's cup ambitions, Boro lifted the FA Amateur Cup for a second time as they defeated Uxbridge 2-0 at Crystal Palace. After five minutes, Uxbridge goalkeeper Gumbrell's punched clearance hit James Kemplay and rebounded in to give the north-east side the lead in calamitous fashion before Bobby Bishop added a second to double the advantage. The following day's match report in *The Referee* questioned 'whether a worse display of football had ever been seen in a final' of the tournament the reporter considered a 'white elephant'. Such concerns mattered not to the jubilant Teesside supporters who made the trip to south London, as the following Monday's *North Eastern Daily Gazette*'s reporter 'Old Bird' exclaimed, 'It is the pleasurable duty of the "Old Bird" to chronicle the fact that with the Middlesbrough club rests the honour of being the champion amateur organisation in all England,' before going on to describe the Boro fans present as 'small in number but strong in lung power'.

23RD APRIL 1910

Tim Williamson was an unlikely goal hero – as of August 2024 the only goalkeeper to score a league goal for the club – after he converted a spot kick as Middlesbrough finished their home campaign with a 2-2 draw against Liverpool. George Elliott was Boro's other goalscorer, adding his fourth of the campaign in his debut season.

23RD APRIL 2006

Boro headed to Villa Park to face West Ham United for a place in the FA Cup Final. A tight encounter was settled by a Marlon Harewood goal with 12 minutes remaining. Boro pressed for an equaliser and Chris Riggott fluffed his lines inside the box with seconds remaining as he dragged his shot wide of Shaka Hislop's far post.

24TH APRIL 1998

Paul Merson scored after two minutes at Vale Park and Mark Schwarzer made a string of fine saves as Boro held on against Port Vale for a vital three points in their battle for promotion.

25TH APRIL 2015

An incredible seven-goal thriller at Craven Cottage ended in disappointment for Boro as Ross McCormack scored at the death to complete his hat-trick and effectively end the visitors' slim hopes of automatic promotion. With Fulham leading 3-1 through Michael Turner and McCormack (two) – Adam Reach having responded – the game looked over when George Friend was dismissed. Yet a battling response from the ten men saw Daniel Ayala pull a goal back and Kike equalise with two minutes remaining. In search of a winner, boss Aitor Karanka sent goalkeeper Dimi Konstantopoulos forward for a late corner but Fulham broke away to take the points.

26TH APRIL 2017

Boro recorded their first league win of 2017 and pushed Sunderland to the brink of relegation with a 1-0 Tees–Wear derby win at the Riverside. Marten de Roon scored the only goal of the match as the home side recorded their only league double of an ill-fated Premier League campaign.

27TH APRIL 1895

Middlesbrough's first national cup triumph ended in trophyless controversy after the Teessiders defeated Old Carthusians 2-1 to claim the FA Amateur Cup. The Linthorpe Road Ground side's path to FA Amateur Cup glory had seen the Teessiders defeat Bishop Auckland, Darlington, Old Brightonians and the Lancashire Regiment to set up a final against the holders at Headingley. In the build-up, the tie was billed as a clash between north and south with the Middlesbrough press reporting the holders were anxious ahead of the final in the north. The match itself brought an early example of a 'typical Boro' experience, with the path to glory proving anything but straightforward. With the game goalless at half-time, captain Bach missed a glorious chance to put the Teessiders ahead. Boro then fell behind and as they reeled from the goal it seemed as though the title would once again go to the Surrey side. However, Boro slowly regained their composure and as Allport headed towards goal, Mullen charged the keeper to level the scores. The goal spurred on the northern side who had a goal ruled out before, with just two minutes remaining, Nelmes scored a sensational winner to secure 'the blue ribbon of amateur football' for Boro. Upon the team's return to Teesside, the cup winners' arrival at Middlesbrough Station attracted a huge crowd before 'a band preceded the players down Linthorpe Road to the Masham Hotel, the club's headquarters, kept by Tom Bach, the popular captain of the team'. However, there was a major problem – there was no trophy. As club chairman Mr Forrester addressed the assembled faithful, he thanked them for their support before commenting 'in strong terms upon the fact that the Football Association had not seen fit to have the cup at Leeds'. In fact, Old Carthusians still had the trophy after themselves only receiving it a couple of months earlier! The cup did finally make its way to Teesside after some strongly worded correspondence from the Boro officials.

PLAY UP MIDDLESBRO

T. BACH.

CAPTᴺ

JORDISON & CO LTD LONDON & MBRO

27TH APRIL 2006

Lightning does strike twice! Massimo Maccarone's 89th-minute goal sensationally sent Middlesbrough to their first UEFA Cup Final with a 4-3 aggregate win over Steaua Bucharest in only the Teessiders' second season in major European football. The hero from the quarter-final once again helped Boro defy the odds in the most incredible of comebacks. Trailing 1-0 from the first leg in Bucharest, the tie looked as good as over when Nicolae Dică and Dorin Goian capitalised on two fumbled saves from Brad Jones to give the Romanians a 3-0 advantage after just 24 minutes at the Riverside. On 25 minutes, an injured Gareth Southgate was substituted and Maccarone was introduced to the fray. It took the Italian only seven minutes to make an impact as he drilled a powerful shot beyond Carlos in the visitors' goal. With only 27 minutes remaining and needing to score three goals without reply, Mark Viduka headed in from a whipped Stewart Downing cross to bring faint hope. Chris Riggott then gave Boro the lead on the night as he bundled a parried Downing effort over the line with 18 minutes remaining. With less than two minutes left, Boro pushed on and a dream cross from Downing was met by a wonderful header at the back post by Maccarone. The strike prompted commentator Ali Brownlee to declare, 'Boro have struck a stake to the heart of Dracula's boys and it could be Eindhoven time.' A nervy finish followed and Ugo Ehiogu made a stunning block in the box after a mix-up in the home defence as it looked like Steaua might break Boro hearts at the last. However, Boro held on and Brownlee uttered immortal words that now appear on a wall mural en route to the Riverside as a reminder of the much-loved late commentator, 'That is it … it's Eindhoven … it's Eindhoven. Boro have made it. One of the most glorious nights in the history of football. We go back to 1876. The Infant Hercules fathomed out of the foundries of Teesside; mined out of the Eston Hills. We're roaring all the way to Eindhoven and the UEFA Cup Final. It's party! Party! Party! Everybody round my house for a parmo!'

27TH APRIL 1974

The final match of Boro's promotion season pitted Bobby and Jack Charlton against one another in the dugouts at relegated Preston North End. Any suggestion that Jack might have taken pity on his younger brother were quickly dismissed as Boro raced into a 3-0 lead within 25 minutes through goals from Peter Brine, Alan Foggon and John Hickton. Preston pulled two goals back before half-time and as the Lancastrians battled for an equaliser, Middlesbrough found a way through once again as Brine doubled his tally. The 4-2 win meant the visitors finished a memorable campaign with a post-war record 65-point haul.

28TH APRIL 1992

A 2-0 win over Grimsby Town at Ayresome Park left Boro just one win away from promotion and guaranteed at least a play-off berth. A Jimmy Phillips penalty and a headed goal from former Mariner Paul Wilkinson were enough to put Lennie Lawrence's men on the brink of a place in the inaugural Premier League.

29TH APRIL 1967

John Hickton scored a hat-trick and John O'Rourke grabbed the other as Stan Anderson's men powered to a 4-0 win over promotion rivals Torquay United at Ayresome Park. The victory renewed hope that Boro would complete a remarkable turnaround by winning promotion back to the second tier at the first time of asking despite spending nearly half the campaign in the bottom half of the table.

30TH APRIL 1974

Jack Charlton – The Boss, a documentary filmed the previous year as the Middlesbrough manager prepared his side ahead of a scheduled clash with his brother Bobby's Preston North End at Ayresome Park, was aired on BBC 1.

30TH APRIL 1995

Boro played their final league match at Ayresome Park with Luton Town the visitors for the last home fixture clash of the First Division campaign. A sell-out 23,903 crowd packed into the famous old ground ahead of kick-off as dozens of Boro legends from across the decades paraded around the pitch before the Riverside Stadium was revealed as the winner of a fans' poll as the name for Middlesbrough's new home at Middlehaven. The other options were Erimus, Middlehaven, and Teesside Stadium. Despite Luton having little to play for, it was far from plain sailing for Bryan Robson's men. Boro's £1m defender Neil Cox spurned the chance to give the home side the lead when his penalty was saved by youngster Kelvin Davis in the Hatters' goal. However, Boro were not to be denied and John Hendrie put them ahead on the stroke of half-time. John Taylor's headed equaliser in the second half threatened to spoil the party before Hendrie scored in front of the Holgate. That goal ultimately proved to be both the winner on the day and – with results later in the week going Boro's way – the strike that secured promotion back to the top flight. At the final whistle, dozens of Boro fans filed on to the pitch before the players acknowledged the supporters as Ayresome Park said goodbye to league football.

MIDDLESBROUGH
On This Day

MAY

1st MAY 1994

Lennie Lawrence's last match as Boro boss ended in defeat at Ayresome Park with Gareth Southgate the star man in Crystal Palace's 3-2 victory. The game encapsulated the season as Boro impressed at times but faltered all too easily. After Richard Liburd had given the home side the lead, Southgate equalised before a comedy of errors in the Boro defence eventually saw Stephen Pears parry into the path of David Whyte. Paul Wilkinson equalised before the break but Palace pushed on to win the game courtesy of a Chris Armstrong goal to secure the First Division title as they looked forward to the following season in the top flight.

2nd MAY 1970

Boro made their competitive European football bow as they defeated European Cup Winners' Cup semi-finalists Roma – knocked out on the toss of a coin following a draw with Górnik Zabrze before the days of penalty shoot-outs to decide the outcome. In front of 14,196 at Ayresome Park, John Hickton's second-half free kick proved enough to give Stan Anderson's side a 1-0 win over a Roma team featuring future England manager Fabio Capello. There was press cynicism towards both the tournament and the visitors with football journalist Ken Gorman, after praising youngster Fausto Landini, declaring, 'As for the rest ... Sophia Loren would have more impact on Bill Gates and company. It would have been a far more alluring spectacle, too, come to that!'

2nd MAY 1992

Despite a pre-match fire, booby traps that had put the fixture in doubt, going a goal down and having a man sent off, Lennie Lawrence's Boro gained promotion with a 2-1 win over Wolves at Molineux. The game burst into life on 65 minutes when Nicky Mohan was sent off and a minute later Andy Mutch put the home side ahead. Seven minutes later the visitors equalised through Jon Gittens – a goal incorrectly credited to Bernie Slaven in that night's *Sports Gazette*. It was left to Paul Wikinson to grab the winner on 77 minutes with a characteristic header that secured promotion. At the end of the match there were jubilant scenes as many of the 5,000 travelling fans celebrated with the players on the pitch as they looked forward to top-flight football in the inaugural Premier League season.

2ND MAY 1994

With league gates having dropped below 10,000 – in one instance hitting as low as 6,286 – and with fans calling for the manager's exit, Lennie Lawrence parted ways with Middlesbrough after three years in charge. An announcement issued by the club stated, 'Our aim now is to develop a team that will consistently excite and entertain the supporters and persuade those who have perhaps missed a few games in the last few seasons to return.'

3RD MAY 1986

Boro arrived at Gay Meadow needing a win and hoping that results elsewhere went their way to avoid only their second relegation to the third tier of English football. Amid crowd trouble, things did not start well with Shrewsbury Town taking the lead in the first half. Despite an Archie Stephens equaliser, Boro were unable to find a way through as the Shrews grabbed a late winner. Ultimately, the result proved academic as Blackburn Rovers' final-day victory over Grimsby Town ensured they finished in 19th place just above the relegation zone with an unassailable four-point lead over Boro.

3RD MAY 1998

Bryan Robson's men made an immediate return to the Premier League with a 4-1 win over Oxford United that secured second place at the expense of rivals Sunderland. The tension on Teesside was palpable as Boro and the U's ended the first half goalless, with Sunderland leading at Swindon Town and sitting in the last automatic promotion spot. However, Middlesbrough rallied in the second half and braces from Alun Armstrong and Craig Hignett – playing his last game for the club – condemned the Black Cats to the uncertainty of the play-offs.

4TH MAY 1929

So impressive was Boro's promotion push during the 1928/29 campaign, the final game – a top-of-the-table clash with Grimsby Town – brought together the two top sides purely to determine who would finish top and with it claim the Second Division championship. The Mariners were cast aside in the showpiece occasion at Ayresome Park as George Camsell grabbed a brace and Owen Williams hit the other in a comprehensive 3-0 win as 36,503 fans – double the last home gate – turned out to share in the special day. After the final whistle, the excitement of the supporters could not be contained as they flooded on to the pitch to congratulate their promotion heroes. The *North Eastern Daily Gazette* hailed Boro as 'a real championship team', and described the club as having 'gone back to the first division in a blaze of glory'. Even the mayors of Middlesbrough, West Hartlepool and Redcar – travelling on the Adriatic – found time to send their 'hearty congratulations' to the club.

4TH MAY 1953

Brian Clough signed his first professional contract for Middlesbrough after the youngster – already on the club's books – had been in scintillating form in local football. Earlier that year Clough's goalscoring exploits for Great Broughton featured in the local press on several occasions. In January, the *Cleveland Standard* reported how Clough grabbed a hat-trick – with his brothers also adding three goals – in a 10-0 home triumph over Skinningrove Works. Less than two months before signing professionally, Clough hit the headlines once again with a seven-goal haul in a 12-1 win over Dunsdale. A month before the striker signed professional forms, following a hat-trick in April 1953, the local press writer declared Clough 'is no doubt a rough diamond with a very bright prospect at centre forward … Add this to the fact that he lives in Middlesbrough, he may well turn out another George Elliott after he has completed his National Service'.

5TH MAY 1971

Nobby Stiles switched Old Trafford for Ayresome Park as Stan Anderson took a £20,000 gamble on the England World Cup winner, who had suffered a difficult spell with a knee injury at Manchester United.

5TH MAY 1990

Battling relegation to the third tier, Boro needed a win in the Tees–Tyne derby and for Bournemouth to fail to beat Leeds United to avoid a second successive demotion. Meanwhile, visitors Newcastle United knew that a win along with favourable results elsewhere would secure promotion to the top flight. After a first-half stalemate, Bernie Slaven opened the scoring before former Newcastle loanee Ian Baird doubled Middlesbrough's lead. Owen McGee unluckily deflected in to give the Magpies hope before Baird and 'The Wolfman' Slaven made sure of the three points. A 1-0 win at Bournemouth for Leeds saw the Yorkshiremen crowned Second Division champions and ensured Boro's survival with the Cherries instead occupying the final relegation spot.

5TH MAY 1996

The Riverside Stadium played host to the visit of a Manchester United side needing a win to make sure of the Premier League title or, in the words of Kevin Keegan, having 'to go to Middlesbrough and get something'. Unfortunately for King Kev – and to the understated delight of many Boro fans in attendance – the visitors ran out 3-0 winners and lifted the trophy on the Riverside pitch as the St James' trophy cabinet remained empty once again.

6TH **MAY 1953**

Graeme Souness, one of Middlesbrough's heroes of Jack Charlton's promotion side of 1974, was born in Edinburgh. He went on to captain Scotland, win a host of domestic and European trophies and was voted Boro's greatest ever player in a players' poll by the club.

6TH **MAY 1981**

After weeks of speculation, Middlesbrough released a statement confirming the departure of manager John Neal by mutual consent after he 'did not wish to accept the new arrangements for the re-organisation that will be implemented at Ayresome Park'. The move came despite the club sitting in a comfortable mid-table position in the top flight and having enjoyed a good cup run. Having been offered the Wrexham job, Neal instead took up the reins at Chelsea at the end of May.

6TH **MAY 1987**

An incredible campaign back from the brink saw Boro secure a return to the Second Division with a game to spare. Wigan Athletic were the visitors to Ayresome Park – their first match at the ground – as an entertaining goalless encounter ensured the home side recorded the point to gain promotion at the first time of asking. Even before the final whistle was blown, hundreds had poured on to the pitch. With news that rivals Swindon Town had drawn and Boro were up come what may, a brief restart and almost immediate final whistle saw the teams sprint to the changing rooms and thousands invade the pitch. After the match Bruce Rioch's men appeared in the directors' box to take the accolade of, and to recognise the backing they had received from, supporters who had stuck by the club during the dark days just nine months earlier.

7TH **MAY 1973**

In curious circumstances, Middlesbrough chairman George Winney confirmed the appointment of England World Cup winner Jack Charlton as the club's manager. The announcement was made at the testimonial match for Harold Shepherdson – the man who had trained the Ashington-born centre-half during England's 1966 triumph – while Charlton himself was playing in his own testimonial against Glasgow Celtic at Elland Road as 34,963 supporters paid tribute to the departing bedrock of the Peacocks' defence.

7TH MAY 2016

Cristhian Stuani's first-half goal ultimately proved enough to ensure it was Boro who were promoted from the Championship rather than Brighton & Hove Albion on a dramatic day at the Riverside. Needing a point against the Seagulls in the final game of the season, with the away side needing a win to move above Boro in the second automatic promotion spot, the Uruguayan opened the scoring in the 19th minute after turning in David Nugent's ball across the box. Dale Stephens turned from hero to villain when he equalised for the visitors ten minutes into the second half but he was then sent off just four minutes later. Despite chances at both ends, there were to be no more goals and as the final whistle blew to confirm promotion, thousands of fans flocked on to the pitch to celebrate a return to the Premier League after a seven-year absence.

8TH MAY 1973

Jack Charlton, celebrating his 38th birthday, wasted no time in stamping his authority at Ayresome Park on his first day in charge. According to one newspaper report, the new gaffer arranged a meeting with his players at a Teesside hotel where he 'told the players the score', while in an interview with the press he suggested a ruthless outlook from the new leader: 'They [Middlesbrough] have some good players, some bad players and some lazy players. What I want to ensure is that some people don't sell me short on effort. I can tolerate poor performances, but not players failing to try their best.'

8TH MAY 1994

John Pickering temporarily took charge of Boro after the departure of Lennie Lawrence as the Teessiders produced a remarkable end-of-season goalfest at The Valley, running out 5-2 winners against Charlton Athletic. Paul Wilkinson opened the scoring just over a minute into the match, with his strike partner John Hendrie grabbing a hat-trick and Jamie Pollock scoring the visitors' last goal of the season in the 84th minute.

9TH MAY 1929

Boro pair George Camsell and John Peacock made their international debuts in England's 4-1 win over France at the Colombes Stadium, with Camsell scoring two of the visitors' goals.

10TH MAY 1947

Captained by Boro left-back George Hardwick, Great Britain defeated the Rest of Europe 6-1 in the 'Match of the Century' at Hampden Park. His Middlesbrough team-mate Wilf Mannion scored twice for Great Britain in front of 134,000 in Glasgow and was only denied a hat-trick when Tommy Lawton kicked the ball into the net on the line after the Boro man 'had beat the defence and pushed the ball almost to the goal line'.

10TH MAY 2006

The biggest game in Middlesbrough FC's history ended in disappointment as Sevilla ran out 4-0 winners in the UEFA Cup Final in Eindhoven. Initially allocated 9,200 tickets for the showpiece occasion, thousands more Boro fans made the trip to the Netherlands and found their way into the Philips Stadion. The Spaniards dominated the contest, with Luís Fabiano opening the scoring after 27 minutes from an unchallenged header. Into the second half the Andalusians continued to press although Boro did have a couple of notable chances, including a close-range effort that Mark Viduka failed to convert and a speculative attempt from half-time substitute Massimo Maccarone that Andrés Palop had to turn round the post. As Boro pushed for an equaliser, Yakubu replaced Franck Queudrue and the Teessiders had a penalty shout turned down after a push on Viduka. Two minutes later the tie was all but over as Enzo Maresca scored from close range on 74 minutes. The future Leicester City and Chelsea manager added his second nine minutes later and former Spurs forward Frédéric Kanouté added a fourth for Sevilla with two minutes of normal time remaining. Boro's dream of European glory was over after they were outclassed in head coach Steve McClaren's last match before taking over the England manager's job. Boro's UEFA Cup Final line-up: Schwarzer, Parnaby, Riggott, Southgate, Queudrue (Yakubu 70), Morrison (Maccarone 45), Rochemback, Boateng, Downing, Viduka (Cattermole 85), Hasselbaink. Unused subs: Jones, Ehiogu, Parlour, Bates.

11TH MAY 1929

England beat Belgium 5-1 in Brussels with George Camsell, making only his second appearance for the national side, grabbing four goals to take his international tally to six. The ex-miner was joined in the team by Middlesbrough team-mate John Peacock, the last time the pair would play together at international level.

11TH MAY 2008

Boro hit Manchester City for eight in Sven-Göran Eriksson's last game in charge of the Citizens. Reduced to ten men following the dismissal of Richard Dunne for bringing down Tuncay Şanlı in the box, Stewart Downing scored the first of his two goals by converting the 15th-minute penalty. An Afonso Alves hat-trick accompanied by goals from Jérémie Aliadière, Adam Johnson and a stunning Fábio Rochemback free kick took the home side's total to eight as they posted their record Premier League win. For City, the defeat equalled their second-heaviest league losses, including the most recent seven-goal defeat at Molineux in 1962. For Boro, the 8-1 win created an optimism for the following campaign that turned out to be woefully misplaced, with the match proving to be the final appearances for key players George Boateng, Rochemback, Mark Schwarzer and Luke Young, some of whom the club failed to adequately replace.

12TH MAY 1951

Partizan Belgrade visited Ayresome Park to take on the home side as Festival of Britain fixtures were played across the nation. The Slavs were 3-2 winners in the second match of their mini-tour of Yorkshire, which also included a 3-2 victory at Hull and 2-0 loss at Bradford Park Avenue.

12TH MAY 1981

Having been strongly linked to the role by the press, Bobby Murdoch was unanimously appointed Middlesbrough's new manager by the club's board, stepping up from his role as youth team coach.

13TH MAY 1994

The *Hartlepool Mail* reported that the 'Bryan Robson for Boro saga' was set to continue over the weekend, although reports elsewhere indicated the Manchester United legend had already agreed to take over as player-manager at Ayresome Park on a £200,000-a-year deal. Other sources had suggested that Robbo was ready to make an unlikely switch from Old Trafford to join Manchester City.

14TH MAY 1970

Boro's first competitive European fixture on the continent, scheduled to take place at the Olympic Stadium against Roma, was postponed in chaotic circumstances owing to a strike by the Italian Olympic Committee. The rescheduled tie was held at Rome's Stadio Flaminio two days later – an athletics meeting was taking place at the original venue – and ended 1-1.

14TH MAY 1996

Middlesbrough unveiled new Brazilian signing Emerson to hundreds of fans gathered outside the Riverside after the Portuguese league's player of the year completed a £4m switch from Bobby Robson's Porto.

15TH MAY 2005

Qualification for a second season of European football went down to the final game of 2004/05 at the City of Manchester Stadium as Boro and Manchester City battled it out for a place in the following campaign's UEFA Cup. Boro needed only a point and Jimmy Floyd Hasselbaink's stunning first-half free kick put them in the driving seat before Kiki Musampa equalised for the hosts immediately after half-time. In an extraordinary turn of events, City manager Stuart Pearce – despite having striker Jon Macken on the bench – opted to bring on goalkeeper Nicky Weaver for midfielder Claudio Reyna and play David James up front in a pre-planned move. The audacious decision almost paid off for the Citizens as Franck Queudrue handled in the box as the ball headed towards the back post with James lurking. Robbie Fowler stepped up to take the injury-time penalty but Boro stopper Mark Schwarzer guessed correctly to make the save and with it secure another season on the continent for the Teessiders, prompting 'Voice of the Boro' Ali Brownlee to exclaim, 'Mark Schwarzer saves it ... Get in, get in you big Aussie. He's done it, I could plant a kiss on his forehead. Mark Schwarzer saved it. Mark Schwarzer to the left-hand side. He's the greatest Australian hero since Ned Kelly, marvellous stuff.'

16TH MAY 1918

Wilf Mannion was born in South Bank, the son of Irish migrants Thomas and Mary Mannion. The St Peter's RC School pupil would go on to become one of the greatest footballers ever as he starred for England, Great Britain and Middlesbrough. Mannion's Irish heritage provoked a strong reaction from his father after the Boro star set up Tom Finney for the winner in England's first international against the Republic of Ireland in 1946. In his biography, Mannion recalled, 'When I got back my father called me all the names under the sun, what with me making the goal for Finney to score. He was listening to it on the radio ... He says, "You were the bloody luckiest team in the world. They were all over you" – and he was right.'

16TH MAY 1967

'Give us a goal, John O'Rourke' was the hat-trick hero as Middlesbrough beat Oxford United 4-1 at Ayresome Park to secure an immediate return to the second tier. John Hickton scored the home side's other goal – all of which came from headers – in front of an official attendance of 39,683. At full time, an estimated 10,000 fans poured on to the pitch from the packed stands and a wall collapsed – 14 people were hurt – as excitement briefly turned to panic but the incident was dealt with and celebrations continued into the night.

16TH MAY 1995

Stephen Pears' testimonial provided an opportunity for Boro to say goodbye to not only one of the club's greatest goalkeepers but also the famous old ground. His Boro Select XI – also featuring Peter Beardsley – defeated the current season's promotion side 3-1. It was left to Pears to score the final goal in front of nearly 20,000 fans as he stepped up to take a penalty in the final minutes to provide a fitting end to a celebratory night during which Boro paraded the First Division trophy.

16TH MAY 1999

Boro suffered a heavy 4-0 defeat at West Ham United as the Hammers secured Intertoto Cup qualification on the final day of the season. The result meant the Teessiders finished their first campaign back in the Premier League in ninth place with 51 points.

17TH MAY 1974

Jack Charlton was named as English football's Manager of the Year, with the Boro boss presented with a £1,000 cheque at a luncheon in Glasgow after pipping Boro-born Don Revie to the title by just one vote out of the 25 cast by journalists. The result did not go down well with the *Liverpool Echo*'s Michael Charters, who dedicated half of the newspaper's back page to making the case for the deposed Bill Shankly's claim while playing down Charlton's achievement.

17TH MAY 1997

Boro's first – and to date only – FA Cup Final appearance ended in a 2-0 defeat to Chelsea in an emotionally charged Wembley as Teesside supporters vociferously decried the three points deduction that had ultimately condemned them to relegation just six days earlier. Roberto Di Matteo scored the then fastest ever FA Cup Final goal, after just 43 seconds, as he fired in from long range beyond the flailing Ben Roberts. Fabrizio Ravanelli limped off on 21 minutes as things went from bad to worse for Boro. It was apparent it would not be their day shortly before half-time when Gianluca Festa's header was incorrectly ruled out for offside. Late in the second half Eddie Newton added the Blues' second to give Ruud Gullit's Chelsea their first FA Cup success since 1970.

18TH MAY 1918

After a stalemate in front of 15,000 at Newcastle United's St James' Park, around 22,000 supporters turned out at Ayresome Park for the Munitionettes Cup Final replay as Blyth Spartans Ladies claimed a 5-0 win over Bolckow Vaughan South Bank.

18TH MAY 1988

Trailing 2-1 from the play-off semi-final first leg at Bradford City, Bernie Slaven's first-half goal took the tie into extra time on a dramatic night on Teesside. Just a minute into extra time, Gary Hamilton burst through and unleashed an unstoppable shot beyond Paul Tomlinson in the Bantams' goal. Despite chances for both sides, there were no further goals and Boro progressed to a two-legged promotion-relegation play-off final against Chelsea to determine if the Teessiders would go up or if the Londoners would cling on to their place in the top flight.

18TH MAY 1994

Bryan Robson was unveiled as Middlesbrough's new player-manager at Ayresome Park, with the local *Herald & Post* newspaper hailing the appointment as 'the most exciting appointment since Big Jack Charlton breezed into the Boro'. 'Captain Marvel' was given a rousing reception by hundreds of supporters including local schoolchildren armed with red and white balloons as he posed for press photographs and performed keepie-uppies in a suit jacket and shirt paired with Boro shorts and socks.

19TH MAY 1980

Arsenal endured a torrid end to the 1979/80 campaign as Boro piled on the misery of an horrendous spell for the Gunners. The Londoners had lost the FA Cup Final to West Ham nine days earlier and then missed out on European Cup Winners' Cup glory midweek at Heysel after losing 5-4 on penalties to Valencia following a goalless draw. A league win at Wolves prior to arriving at Ayresome Park meant victory over Middlesbrough would have ensured UEFA Cup qualification. John Neal's side failed to read the script, however, and stunned the Highbury outfit with a 5-0 win courtesy of goals from Craig Johnston, David Hodgson, David Armstrong (with a brace on his 350th appearance) and Graham Hedley. The victory ensured Boro finished ninth in the First Division, while Terry Neill's men missed out on a UEFA Cup berth at the expense of Ipswich Town, who would go on to win the tournament the following season.

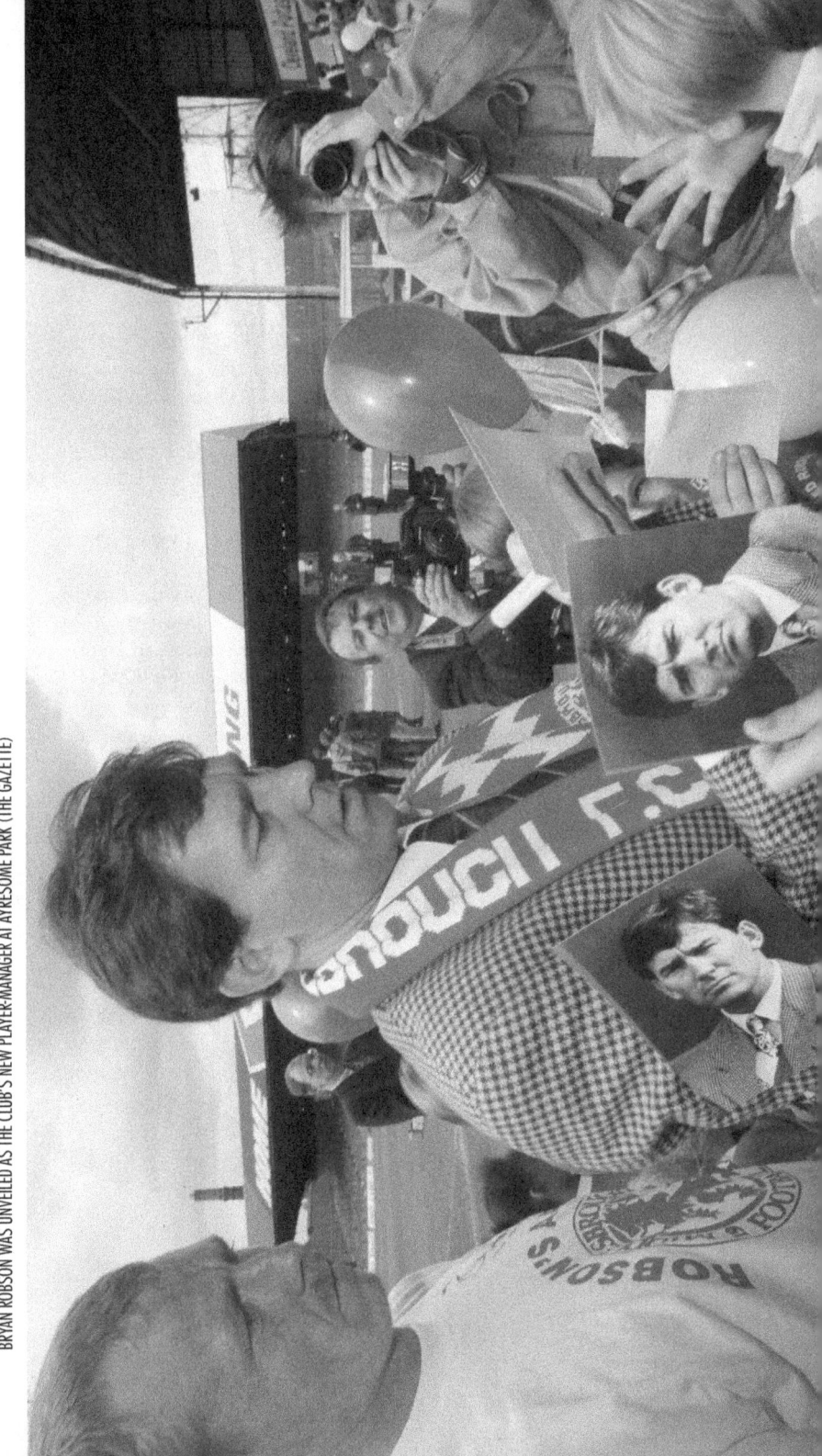

BRYAN ROBSON WAS UNVEILED AS THE CLUB'S NEW PLAYER-MANAGER AT AYRESOME PARK (THE GAZETTE)

19TH MAY 1994

A day after Bryan Robson was unveiled as Boro boss, north of the border the *Daily Record* reported that star striker John Hendrie could be on his way to Glasgow Celtic in an agreed £750,000 deal. However, it was noted that Robson had stated that he wanted to run the rule over players ahead of the new season before agreeing to any transfers.

20TH MAY 1998

The *Daily Mirror* reported that David Platt was set to quit Arsenal and join his old England team-mates Bryan Robson and Paul Gascoigne at newly promoted Middlesbrough in a £2m deal. The midfielder had been linked with a switch to the north-east during the previous season but was said to have been reluctant to drop down into the second tier.

21ST MAY 2000

While the Riverside had become well-established as a venue where Boro fans would go and worship their heroes on a Saturday afternoon, Sunday, 21 May brought a very different type as the Middlesbrough Diocesan Millennium Celebration was held on the hallowed turf. As well as a Millennium Mass, there were dance performances and music from several local artists including celebrated folk singer Vin Garbutt.

22ND MAY 1997

After just one season at the Riverside, the *Daily Mirror* reported that Porto were ready to 'rescue Emerson from his Teesside hell' by re-signing the man they had sold to Middlesbrough just 12 months earlier.

23RD MAY 1996

Nick Barmby all but booked his spot in England's Euro '96 squad as he scored two goals in the Three Lions' 3-0 win over China at the Workers' Stadium in Beijing. Boro's record signing scored a goal in each half, with Paul Gascoigne adding a third, in the first match of a two-game tour of China and Hong Kong better remembered for the infamous 'dentist's chair' tabloid photographs showing England players drinking and partying and which inspired Gazza's famous celebration after scoring against Scotland.

24TH MAY 2009

Needing a minor miracle to extend their 11-year-stay in the Premier League, Gareth Southgate's Boro slumped to a 2-1 defeat at West Ham in a poor display emblematic of a disappointing season. Carlton Cole gave the Hammers the lead before Gary O'Neil's strike provided a glimmer of hope for the travelling Teessiders, but Brad Jones allowed Junior Stanislas's long-range effort to creep into the near post on a bad day for the north-east that also brought relegation for Alan Shearer's Newcastle United at Villa Park.

25TH MAY 1988

Middlesbrough overcame Chelsea in the first leg of the Second Division play-off final first leg courtesy of goals from Trevor Senior and Bernie Slaven in front of a bumper 25,531 crowd that meant Boro had one foot in the First Division and Bobby Campbell's men were facing down the barrel of relegation.

25TH MAY 1996

The *Sports Gazette* front page was adorned with a photograph of Jürgen Klinsmann mocked up in a Boro kit alongside the headline 'Our Kith and Klin' as transfer speculation went into overdrive ahead of Euro '96. Ultimately, there was no Boro switch for the European Championship and World Cup winner as Klinsmann remained at Bayern Munich before returning to Italy with Sampdoria.

25TH MAY 2015

Norwich City triumphed in the Championship play-off final at Wembley courtesy of two early goals in a whirlwind opening 15 minutes. Both teams struck the woodwork – Middlesbrough through a spectacular long-range strike by Jelle Vossen – before the Canaries took the lead on 12 minutes after Cameron Jerome punished indecision by Daniel Ayala in the Teessiders' defence, then Nathan Redmond added a second just three minutes later to condemn Aitor Karanka's men to another season in the second tier.

26TH MAY 2002

Boro skipper Gareth Southgate appeared for England as a substitute as the Three Lions' friendly with Cameroon finished 2-2 in Japan. Future Riverside loan star Geremi was one of the scorers for the Indomitable Lions.

27TH MAY 1895

Following a season of trophy success, one of the issues on the agenda of the Middlesbrough directors' meeting at the Masham Hotel was the question of who would display the cups. It was resolved that Thomas Gibson Poole would remove the Northern League championship cup from his shop window and it be placed in charge of the chairman before the trophy would be placed in the window of Mr Dobinson. The Northern League Cup would be held by vice-chairman Dr Bateman, while the Teesside League Cup would be held by Mr Cubutt.

27TH MAY 2024

Leeds United defender Luke Ayling signed for Boro on a two-year deal with his contract at Elland Road due to expire. Ayling initially moved to Teesside on loan in January 2024 and despite interest from other Championship clubs, the former Yeovil Town man opted for a return to the north-east.

28TH MAY 1988

Two years after almost going out of existence, Boro returned to the top flight following a 2-1 aggregate play-off win over Chelsea. Leading 2-0 from the first leg at Ayresome Park, Gordon Durie's goal was not enough to save the Blues from relegation on home turf in a match marred by crowd trouble and later dubbed the 'Battle of Stamford Bridge'.

29TH MAY 1997

The *Liverpool Echo* reported that Boro boss Bryan Robson was among a list of star names under consideration by the Everton board to fill the vacant manager's post at Goodison Park, with George Graham and Martin O'Neill also linked with the role.

29TH MAY 1997

The *Daily Mirror* reported that Leeds United marksman Brian Deane – whose goal had relegated Middlesbrough at Elland Road just weeks before – was wanted by Bryan Robson as a replacement for want-away Italian Fabrizio Ravanelli. Ultimately, a deal for Deane failed to materialise that summer but the former Sheffield United star did eventually sign for the club in 1998.

TONY MOWBRAY IN ACTION AT STAMFORD BRIDGE IN THE PLAY-OFF AGAINST CHELSEA (THE GAZETTE)

30TH MAY 1988

As national back-page headlines condemned the behaviour of Chelsea fans at Stamford Bridge two days earlier in their play-off aggregate loss to Middlesbrough, newly promoted Boro were given a boost when Gary Pallister declared that he was staying put at Ayresome Park despite rumoured interest from Liverpool and Manchester United.

31ST MAY 1908

Boro defeated a Danish XI 5-2 as the Teessiders finished the season with visits to Denmark and Prague. The trip to Prague brought an amusing incident when, due to a misunderstanding, the Middlesbrough side were without funds. The day was saved when club chairman and mayor of Middlesbrough Thomas Gibson Poole visited a Bohemian bank to plead with the manager to allow him to cash a cheque and, after presenting the Middlesbrough Municipal Year Book as his identification, he was provided with sufficient funds.

31ST MAY 1980

John Neal's Middlesbrough came back from a goal down to win 3-1 against China in the Japan (Kirin) Cup, doing so without the services of David Armstrong, who had flown to Sydney to make his full international debut in England's 2-1 win over Australia at the Sydney Cricket Ground. Mark Proctor, Graeme Hedley and David Shearer scored Boro's goals in Nagoya as they booked their place in the Tokyo final where they would face the winners of the second semi-final between Espanyol and the Japan national team.

MIDDLESBROUGH
On This Day

JUNE

1st JUNE 1980

The *Sunday Sun* reported that David Mills was heading back to the north-east, with Middlesbrough, Newcastle and Sunderland all interested in signing Britain's first £500,000 footballer from West Bromwich Albion.

2nd JUNE 1977

Middlesbrough's post-season tour of Australia made the news back home in England for all the wrong reasons as rival fans clashed at a friendly against South Australia in Adelaide. Reports said supporters fought with each other and the police, with bystanders also subject to harassment and bottles thrown at shop windows. Alf Woods scored both of Boro's goals in a 2-1 win.

2nd JUNE 2001

The *Daily Express* reported that Middlesbrough were chasing Roma star Gabriel Batistuta. Boro had shown a serious interest in Batigol in 1997 when the striker was at Fiorentina but any move was ruled out after relegation to the second tier. According to the latest reports, the Argentina international had grown frustrated in Rome and was keen on a move to England with Chelsea also linked. Ultimately, Batistuta remained in Italy before finishing his playing career with Doha's Al-Arabi.

3rd JUNE 1980

There was cup glory for John Neal's men in Asia as they lifted the Japan (Kirin) Cup after defeating Espanyol on penalties following a 1-1 draw in Tokyo. Craig Johnston scored the game's opening goal with a long-range screamer but the Spaniards equalised and thought they had a winner but were denied by a goal-line save – despite furious protests that saw one of the Espanyol players grab the referee. Tony McAndrew scored the decisive penalty in a 4-3 shoot-out success.

3rd JUNE 2024

Head coach Michael Carrick signed a new deal at Middlesbrough to keep the former Manchester United midfielder at the Riverside for another three years.

4th JUNE 1997

Liverpool were the latest club linked with a move for Boro star Juninho following the club's relegation to the First Division, with the *Daily Mirror* reporting that the Brazilian had told Roy Evans that Anfield was his first-choice destination if his move to Atlético Madrid collapsed.

JOHN NEAL'S SIDE ENJOYED KIRIN CUP GLORY AS THEY DEFEATED ESPANYOL ON PENALTIES IN TOKYO.

5TH JUNE 1977

Boro trounced the Socceroos 5-0 at the Sydney Sports Ground in the latest match of their tour of Australia. John Hickton scored a brace with Tony McAndrew, Willie Maddren and Graeme Souness also scoring in a win that brought scathing criticism of the Australian side in the press.

6TH JUNE 1977

A busy schedule for Boro continued in Australia as the visitors defeated Wollongong City at the Woonona Oval, coming back from a goal down to eventually win 2-1 with substitute John Hickton scoring the winner with four minutes remaining as he continued his goalscoring streak on tour.

6TH JUNE 1991

The fallout from Boro's failure to win promotion via the play-offs weeks earlier saw 11 players placed on the transfer list, including marksmen Ian Baird and Bernie Slaven, as well as defenders Colin Cooper, Alan Kernaghan and Gary Parkinson.

7TH JUNE 1958

Ayresome Park played host to acclaimed basketball stars the Harlem Globetrotters as they clashed with the US Star Basketeers. The event also included six international variety acts and the Dagenham Girl Pipers.

7TH JUNE 1962

North Ormesby lad Alan Peacock made his England debut at the 1962 World Cup in Chile as the Three Lions played out a goalless draw with Bulgaria. The Boro forward was among the action from the off and after eight minutes played a through ball to Jimmy Greaves, who could not make the most of the chance. Peacock might have won the game for England in the second half but failed to convert his snap header from a Ron Flowers cross.

8TH JUNE 1940

The *North Eastern Daily Gazette* reported that Wilf Mannion was 'fit and well' after rumours had spread around the safety of the South Bank-born Boro star who had been serving with the British Expeditionary Force in France.

8TH JUNE 1977

John Neal's side continued their impressive form in Australia as they hammered part-timers Lithgow FC 10-0. John Hickton and Billy Woof scored hat-tricks with Phil Boersma, Graeme Hedley, Alan Walsh and Alf Wood also among the goals.

8TH JUNE 2006

Having been linked with a string of coaches from across the globe, Middlesbrough turned to captain Gareth Southgate as successor to Steve McClaren. Retiring from his playing role at the club, Southgate signed a five-year deal as boss and immediately set to work in securing his own replacement at centre-back, reportedly setting a deadline for Chelsea defender Robert Huth to make a decision on signing ahead of the World Cup kicking off the following day. Boro would have to wait over two months before the German international finally moved to the Riverside.

9TH JUNE 2017

Middlesbrough confirmed the appointment of former Leeds United head coach Garry Monk as the new boss at the Riverside. Boro swooped for the ex-Swansea City man after he failed to reach an agreement on a new contract at Elland Road.

10TH JUNE 2006

Stewart Downing was a second-half replacement for Michael Owen as England laboured to a 1-0 win over Paraguay in their opening match of the 2006 World Cup in Frankfurt.

11TH JUNE 2003

A crowd of 34,000 packed into the Riverside Stadium as the venue played host to the senior England team for the first time with Slovakia the visitors for a Euro 2004 qualifier. Boro's Gareth Southgate and Szilárd Németh were on opposing sides as the stand-in skipper, winning his 50th cap, grabbed a brace in a 2-1 victory.

12TH JUNE 2001

Highly rated Manchester United assistant manager Steve McClaren was appointed Middlesbrough boss, with the club beating off interest from Southampton and West Ham United to secure the former Derby first-team coach's signature. At his unveiling, McClaren said, 'The next step in my career was management and I am incredibly excited by the job here at Middlesbrough. I have had a great time at Manchester United, working with a fantastic manager and great players, but as soon as I met the chairman Steve Gibson I had no hesitation in taking up the opportunity.'

MIDDLESBROUGH'S NEW SIGNING GARETH SOUTHGATE WITH NEW MANAGER STEVE McCLAREN FACE THE PRESS.

13TH JUNE 1998

Former Boro man and transfer target Stuart Ripley headed to Southampton after the Saints agreed a £1.5m fee with Blackburn Rovers for the Premier League winner.

14TH JUNE 2024

Delano Burgzorg joined Middlesbrough from Mainz for an undisclosed fee, with the 25-year-old signing a four-year contract on Teesside to complete a return to England after spending the previous season on loan at Huddersfield Town.

15TH JUNE 1994

Bryan Robson convinced Neil Cox to drop down a division to join Middlesbrough from Aston Villa as the Teessiders paid out a £1m club-record transfer fee.

15TH JUNE 1998

The *Daily Record* reported that Bryan Robson was keen to revive his interest in long-term target John Collins. Three years after attempting to lure Collins from Glasgow Celtic, Robbo aimed to convince the Scotland international to make the move from Monaco to Middlesbrough. Robson would ultimately miss out on Collins again as the midfielder instead opted for a move to Everton.

16TH JUNE 1976

Jack Charlton flew to Stockholm to cast an eye over Norway's amateur striker Tom Lund as he led the line against Sweden in a World Cup qualifier – once considered by Ajax as the man to replace Johan Cruyff and linked with Bayern Munich and Real Madrid. Ultimately, no deal materialised and Lund went on to enjoy success with Lillestrøm as the club enjoyed a golden era.

17TH JUNE 1935

Phil Bach, a former player and later a board member of 24 years, decided not to seek re-election as a director at the club's annual meeting owing to commitments with the Football Association. The club reported losses of £660, pointing to inclement weather as the reason for a drop in gate receipts from £18,092 in the previous season to £14,720.

18TH JUNE 1941

Middlesbrough FC's annual accounts revealed losses of £674, with the deficit attributed to wartime conditions and falling gates due to poor weather. Meanwhile, the local press reported that 22 players from the club had joined the forces.

PHIL BACH STEPPED DOWN FROM THE BORO BOARD OWING TO COMMITMENTS WITH THE FA (CULLEY COLLECTION)

18TH JUNE 1995

The *Sunday Sun* reported that Alex Ferguson had targeted England under-21 international Jamie Pollock as a replacement for Italy-bound Paul Ince in the heart of the Manchester United midfield. The combative midfielder remained at Middlesbrough for a season before a Bosman move to Osasuna, although he did eventually move to the north-west with Bolton Wanderers and then Manchester City. In the absence of Pollock, Ferguson turned to youth product Nicky Butt to fill the void left by Ince.

19TH JUNE 1948

Newspapers across the country reported that Boro's star man, Wilf Mannion, was wanted by Arsenal. Mannion, who had made several pleas for a transfer away from Teesside, according to reports, would be the subject of a record bid by Gunners manager Tom Whittaker.

20TH JUNE 2020

The football season resumed following a pause of several months owing to the Covid-19 pandemic. The return to an empty Riverside Stadium was not a happy one for Jonathan Woodgate's men as they were hammered 3-0 by visitors Swansea City.

21ST JUNE 2019

Blackburn Rovers announced the signing of former England international Stewart Downing on a free transfer from Middlesbrough after the Pallister Park lad had made over 400 appearances for his hometown club.

22ND JUNE 1995

As Boro prepared for life back in the top flight, the *Daily Express* reported that Bryan Robson was set to make a move for Liverpool's former England international Mark Wright in a bid to strengthen his side's defence.

23RD JUNE 2020

Following an abysmal run of results, Jonathan Woodgate was dismissed as Boro boss and replaced by the experienced Neil Warnock. Ronnie Jepson and Kevin Blackwell joined Warnock at the Riverside as part of the backroom staff as the former Sheffield United man attempted to steer Boro clear of the drop.

24TH JUNE 2022

Republic of Ireland international defender Darragh Lenihan signed for Boro on a four-year deal after his contract at Blackburn Rovers – where he had been captain – had expired.

25TH JUNE 1991

Manager Colin Todd walked out on the club after a string of disagreements with the board. The directors' refusal to sanction the appointment of Martin Harvey as youth team coach proved to be the breaking point for the former Derby County and England star, who had been assistant to Bruce Rioch before his own 15-month stint in charge at Ayresome Park.

25TH JUNE 1999

The *Evening Gazette* reported that Bryan Robson was ready to go close to matching Ipswich's £6m asking price for Kieron Dyer. The England squad man had been linked to several Premier League clubs including Leeds United. The move for the Tractor Boys star came as Middlesbrough were trying to complete a deal for Wolves' Robbie Keane and were linked with AC Milan defender Christian Ziege. Ultimately, it would be to Tyneside rather than Teesside that Dyer headed as he completed a move to Newcastle United in July 1999. It would not be until January 2013 that Dyer would eventually join Boro, signing on a short-term deal during former Ipswich team-mate Tony Mowbray's tenure as Boro boss. However, Boro did complete a deal for Ziege that summer and, while they missed out on Keane as a player, the Irish international joined the coaching staff at the Riverside Stadium in June 2019, working alongside new gaffer Jonathan Woodgate.

26TH JUNE 1998

Hámilton Ricard was helpless to stop England storming to a 2-0 victory over Colombia at the 1998 World Cup in France. The South Americans were already trailing by two goals when Boro's frontman came on to try and inspire an unlikely comeback in Lens, although Ricard did manage a speculative curled effort that went wide in one of Los Cafeteros' rare attacks.

27TH JUNE 1954

Wilf Mannion announced his decision to retire from football, bringing to an end 18 years with Middlesbrough. In a letter to the club, the former England and Great Britain star stated that he would not be re-signing at Ayresome Park. The news shocked the football world as Mannion still ranked among the top inside-forwards in the league. Of his decision to end his career aged 36, the South Bank schemer asked, 'What is the good of going right to the end of the line? I have nothing in mind and nothing in particular in view for the future, but something will turn up.' By the end of the year, Mannion had reversed his decision to retire and returned to professional football for a brief spell with Hull City.

27TH JUNE 2020

New boss Neil Warnock guided Boro to a 2-0 win at Stoke City in his first game in charge following the departure of Jonathan Woodgate. It was only the club's second win in 13 games. Ashley Fletcher and substitute Marcus Tavernier were the goal heroes as Boro climbed two points clear of the bottom three.

28TH JUNE 1990

Despite having days earlier turned down a move to Ayresome Park to remain at Leeds United, press reports suggested that former Newcastle United man John Hendrie had been tempted by improved terms and was set to join Boro in a £500,000 switch from Elland Road.

29TH JUNE 1950

Wilf Mannion – tipped in the press to be a star man of the tournament – was on the wrong end of one of the greatest ever World Cup upsets as a star-studded England side lost 1-0 to USA in Brazil. Mannion would later recall, 'It was shooting practice for all of us. They were getting fed and I was hitting balls too, but it just wouldn't go in. Not for any of us.'

30TH JUNE 2002

Former Boro man Juninho made a substitute appearance for Brazil as the Samba Boys defeated Germany 2-0 in the final of the 2002 World Cup in Yokohama.

MIDDLESBROUGH
On This Day

JULY

1st JULY 1895

The meeting of the club's directors brought an unusual resolution when it was resolved 'that no horses be allowed to graze in [the] Football Field for [the] remainder of the non-playing season'.

2nd JULY 2022

Chris Wilder's team kicked off their pre-season at Bishop Auckland's Heritage Park. Boro led 2-0 at the break through goals from Riley McGree and new boy Tommy Smith. Anfernee Dijksteel added a third early in the second half before an own goal and a Josh Coburn strike with 15 minutes remaining completed the rout.

3rd JULY 1990

Oxford United's promising 21-year-old midfielder Robbie Mustoe completed a £375,000 move to Middlesbrough, while John Hendrie also completed the details of his on-off transfer from Leeds United. Mustoe would go on to make 367 appearances for the club during a 12-year stay on Teesside, while Hendrie would secure his place in history as the last league goalscorer at Ayresome Park.

3rd JULY 2002

Boro completed the signing of highly rated Italian striker Massimo Maccarone from Empoli for £8.15m to smash the club's transfer record. The youngster had impressed the coaching team at Middlesbrough during the summer's European Under-21 Championship, where he scored a brace for Italy against England.

4th JULY 1996

Juventus's Champions League Final goalscorer Fabrizio Ravanelli completed a club record £7m move to Middlesbrough from the Stadio Delle Alpi. The Italian international's four-year deal turned the attention of the national media to the north-east as news of ambitious Boro's latest signing appeared on back pages across the country. The *Daily Mirror* dedicated a whole section of the following day's newspaper to providing a 'Welcome to Middlesbrough' guide that sneeringly declared, 'Ravanelli will know when he has reached Middlesbrough when he spots the ICI chimneys and the smoke that often hangs over the town.'

5th JULY 1994

Sheffield Wednesday defender Nigel Pearson completed a move to Middlesbrough for £500,000 (rising to £750,000 after appearances) as Bryan Robson continued to add experience to his squad ahead of his first season in charge. Pearson was Robson's third signing with Clayton Blackmore and Neil Cox having already put pen to paper at Ayresome Park. The former Hillsborough skipper was immediately installed as Boro captain.

5TH JULY 2019

Jonathan Woodgate's first match as Boro boss ended in defeat in Austria as Graz AK ran out 2-0 winners in a pre-season friendly at the Christof Industries Arena.

6TH JULY 2006

Gareth Southgate revealed that he had decided to release Brazilian midfield maestro Doriva to make space in the squad to allow young starlets Lee Cattermole and Josh Walker to progress and gain experience in the centre of the midfield.

7TH JULY 1997

Boro unveiled new signing Paul Merson as they pulled off an incredible coup in luring the 29-year-old Arsenal playmaker to the north-east in a £4.5m deal. With Arsène Wenger having made it clear that Merson did not feature in his plans, the England international opted to rebuild his career at Middlesbrough. The move proved beneficial for both player and club as the 'Magic Man' starred in Boro's promotion campaign and won a recall to the England squad in his only full season on Teesside.

7TH JULY 2004

Dutch international defender Michael Reiziger revealed that he had chosen to join Middlesbrough ahead of Spanish giants Valencia after completing his move from Barcelona to Boro.

7TH JULY 2017

Norwich City's Jonny Howson and Derby County defender Cyrus Christie completed permanent moves to Middlesbrough for undisclosed fees to become new manager Garry Monk's first signings. Christie's stay proved to be brief and he left after less than seven months on Teesside, while Howson went on to captain the club and was a key player in the Boro midfield for over seven years.

8TH JULY 2004

Mark Viduka arrived at Rockcliffe after completing his move from relegated Leeds United. Signed for £4.5m, the Australian international impressed during a three-year stay on Teesside that included starring in the run to the UEFA Cup Final in 2006.

9TH JULY 1923

Manager Jimmy Howie, in his post since 1920, resigned from his role at Middlesbrough after rejecting the re-engagement terms offered by the club.

9TH JULY 2004

New signing Jimmy Floyd Hasselbaink was at Rockcliffe as Steve McClaren pulled off a sensational deal to bring the Dutch international to Teesside on a free transfer switch from Chelsea.

10TH JULY 1991

Charlton Athletic manager Lennie Lawrence was confirmed as the new boss of Middlesbrough after weeks of speculation over who would replace the departed Colin Todd. Chairman Colin Henderson promised the new manager over £1m to spend in the summer to improve the squad, which had suffered play-off heartbreak the previous season.

10TH JULY 2020

The football world was in mourning as it was announced that England 1966 World Cup winner Jack Charlton had died, aged 85. From 1973 to 1977 in his first job in management, Charlton guided Boro to promotion to the top flight in his first season in charge, won the Anglo-Scottish Cup, led his side to the League Cup semi-finals and established Middlesbrough in the First Division. He returned to the club in 1984 to help steer Boro clear of relegation before departing for a final time that summer.

11TH JULY 1996

According to reports in Argentina, Bryan Robson had made an audacious £11.5m move for Fiorentina hitman Gabriel Batistuta to partner new signing Fabrizio Ravanelli up front. Elsewhere, the press in the Midlands linked Jan Åge Fjørtoft – likely to fall down the pecking order at the Riverside – with a move to Birmingham City.

11TH JULY 1999

Boro's goalscoring star Hámilton Ricard led the line for Colombia but failed to get on the scoresheet as they crashed out of the Copa América at the quarter-final stage as Chile triumphed 3-2 in Paraguay.

11TH JULY 2001

Gareth Southgate became Steve McClaren's first signing at Middlesbrough as he completed a £6.5 million transfer from Aston Villa. The move meant Southgate was reunited at the Riverside with his former Villa Park defensive partner Ugo Ehiogu.

THE DEATH OF JACK CHARLTON, PICTURED HERE WITH THE DIVISION TWO TROPHY IN 1974, LEFT THE FOOTBALL WORLD IN MOURNING (THE GAZETTE)

12TH JULY 1966

North Korea opened their 1966 World Cup campaign at Ayresome Park with a 3-0 loss to the USSR. Despite initially impressing with their pressing play, the Asians struggled to match the physicality of the USSR with the *Evening Gazette* reporting how the Russians were too tough for the Koreans, who gained the sympathy of the Boro faithful – no doubt relating to the struggling side after their own team's plummet to the third tier of English football.

13TH JULY 1995

The *Daily Express* reported that Bryan Robson was set to raid his former club to secure the signing of winger Andrei Kanchelskis from Manchester United, with Alex Ferguson said to be mulling over the deal. Rather than heading for a Robbo reunion at the Riverside, the Russia international instead opted for a move to Everton.

14TH JULY 1961

Brian Clough departed Ayresome Park in a controversial £45,000 switch to north-east rivals Sunderland. The outspoken star striker, third in the club's all-time top scorers list with 204 goals, moved for less than the £55,000 Boro had hoped for that would have matched the record fee between English clubs paid by Manchester City for Huddersfield Town's Denis Law. During his time on Teesside, Clough caused controversy by criticising his team-mates who leaked goals as easily as he scored them, which ultimately contributed to the entirety of his time at Middlesbrough having been played out in the second tier.

15TH JULY 1966

Following on from a 3-0 defeat to the USSR in their opening World Cup match, North Korea's prospects of progress – or even recording a point – looked ominous as they fell behind to an early Chile penalty at Ayresome Park, a goal greeted with silence from the Boro faithful who had taken the Asians to their hearts. Minutes from elimination, the Koreans sent the crowd into raptures with a late equaliser. The *Evening Gazette*'s Cliff Mitchell captured the emotions of the moment, 'I think it is correct to say that the crowd of 13,792 was as much responsible for the goal as the jubilant little Korean forward. When the equaliser came, some electric strip lighting in the press refreshment room up in the stand at Ayresome Park was brought down by the stamping of a crowd that has well and truly "adopted" the Asians ... Why don't they cheer the Borough like that? ... The Koreans, obviously heartened by the fact that they were cheered every time they were on the ball, attacked with tremendous enthusiasm ... I imagine that there will be quite a good crowd of Borough (or should it be Korea?) supporters at Ayresome Park for the final match against strong favourites Italy next Tuesday.'

16TH JULY 1991

The *Evening Gazette* reported that Ian Baird had played his last game for Boro after turning down an offer from Lennie Lawrence to remain on Teesside. The former Leeds United man – transfer-listed by Colin Todd earlier in the summer prior to his shock departure from the club – was linked with moves to Hearts and Bristol City, with the target man moving to Ashton Gate soon after.

17TH JULY 2000

Paul Gascoigne ended a disappointing spell on Teesside after signing a two-year deal with Everton to reunite with Walter Smith. Gazza impressed in Boro's promotion spell and helped secure safety in the Premier League. There were occasional signs of brilliance but injury problems and challenges off the pitch contributed to the former England man having a limited impact at the Riverside.

17TH JULY 2017

Nottingham Forest's 24-year-old forward Britt Assombalonga joined Middlesbrough for a club-record £15m transfer fee as Garry Monk turned to proven Championship goalscoring experience to spearhead Boro's push for an immediate return to the Premier League.

18TH JULY 1994

Chairman Steve Gibson, having unveiled plans for a new stadium the previous year, revealed further details of the shape of what was to come at the club's new home down by the River Tees. Featuring a horseshoe design, it had a proposed name of Ayresome Boulevard. The initial plans that appeared on the front page of the *Evening Gazette* included a mini stadium and pitches behind the East Stand and a proposed future banqueting suite behind the North Stand.

18TH JULY 2000

Mark Crossley joined Middlesbrough on a free transfer to provide competition for the number one jersey following the departure of Ben Roberts to Charlton Athletic, also on a free. Although Crossley's game time in a Middlesbrough shirt was limited he impressed when called upon, most notably during the 2001/02 season while deputising for the injured Mark Schwarzer in which he kept six clean sheets in 13 league starts alongside three shutouts in the FA Cup.

19TH JULY 1966

Ayresome Park played host to arguably the greatest World Cup shock of all time as Italy exited the tournament. Despite gloomy pre-match predictions of the Koreans' prospects in their final group match against the Azzurri, the Middlesbrough crowd rallied behind the Asian underdogs, drowning out the noise of some 3,000 Italian supporters at Ayresome Park. Italy were reduced to ten men due to an injury to captain Giacomo Bulgarelli – in the days before substitutions – and the North Koreans took full advantage with a Pak Doo-ik strike late in the first half that proved to be the winner. At the final whistle Ayresome Park was in 'uproar' with BBC commentator Frank Bough exclaiming, 'This stadium has never had support like this for years and years.' The *Teesside Star*'s match report led with 'The Mouse That Roared' and hailed the day 'the little Korean lion roared, and for 90 breathtaking minutes out-tackled and out-ran the mighty Italians'. The role of the Middlesbrough support was also highlighted, 'They had an ally in the Boro' crowd, who went wild when the Koreans scored and followed this up with chants of "Easy" and "We want two" to the chagrin of a large, colourful and childish Italian contingent in the crowd ... As the game went on the Italian supporters got more and more quiet, and the home crowd – football foster parents to the Korean team – shouted for more and more ... When the final whistle went the Italians slunk dejectedly from the field while the Korean team and their handful of officials danced and shouted with delight to a standing ovation from the 17,000 crowd.'

20TH JULY 2002

The *Evening Gazette*'s back page was dominated by the news that Boro had completed a deal to sign Cameroon star Geremi on loan from Real Madrid for the forthcoming season. The newspaper reported how Boro had beaten a host of top clubs to complete the signing – including 'cash-strapped' Chelsea, who had failed to raise the £7m finance for a deal earlier in the summer.

21ST JULY 1978

The Newport Jazz Festival turned Ayresome Park into a home of music rather than football. Held over three days, the line-up included headliner Ella Fitzgerald along with Oscar Peterson, Art Blakey, Dizzy Gillespie and numerous other acts.

22ND JULY 1991

It was all change in the full-back positions at Ayresome Park. Colin Cooper departed for Millwall to reunite with former boss Bruce Rioch as Irish defender Curtis Fleming arrived on Teesside looking to impress manager Lennie Lawrence enough to get a deal over the line, having earlier turned down a move to Oldham Athletic.

23RD JULY 2004

Arsenal star Ray Parlour, aka the 'Croydon Pelé', put pen to paper on a three-year deal at Middlesbrough after spending 15 years at Highbury. The England international played a pivotal role as Boro enjoyed two seasons in the UEFA Cup until being released in January 2007 following injury problems.

24TH JULY 2007

Prospective new signing Luke Young looked on from the stands as Boro won 2-0 against Darlington in a pre-season friendly. Darlington-born Tom Craddock scored both goals in a comfortable win for the visitors.

25TH JULY 1995

As Bryan Robson helped unveil Boro's new kit adorned with new sponsor Cellnet, who had also secured a ten-year naming rights deal for the new Riverside Stadium, the *Daily Express*'s John Donoghue revealed that the gaffer had held off on signing a long-term deal with the club for fear management might not be for him in the years to come.

26TH JULY 1992

A crowd of 20,566 turned out for Tony Mowbray's testimonial match as Lennie Lawrence's newly promoted Middlesbrough took on Mogga's new club, Glasgow Celtic. Ending 1-1 with Paul Wilkinson scoring the home side's goal, the occasion is remembered on Teesside for the vast number of Bhoys fans – estimated at 10,000 – who turned the town green and white on the Saturday night ahead of the friendly fixture.

26TH JULY 1981

Ahead of the new season, thousands of supporters attended the first official opening day at Ayresome Park, with proceeds from the entry fees of 20p for adults and 10p for children going to charities involved in the International Year of the Disabled.

26TH JULY 2006

Relegated Sunderland's star man Julio Arca completed a move to Gareth Southgate's Middlesbrough in a £1.75m deal from the club's north-east rivals.

27TH JULY 1998

Boro's pre-season friendly against Stockport County was the unlikely focus of national press attention as Paul Gascoigne made his first appearance since his high-profile axe from Glenn Hoddle's England World Cup squad. Gazza was described in match reports as 'a class above any other player on view' as he starred in a 1-1 draw.

28TH JULY 2000

Having been extensively linked with moves away from Teesside, the *Evening Gazette* reported that Boro were ready to cash in on German international Christian Ziege with Liverpool, Barcelona and Real Madrid all said to be interested in the club's player of the year.

29TH JULY 2023

French outfit AJ Auxerre were the visitors for Michael Carrick's side's final pre-season friendly ahead of the new season. The French outfit led 2-0 with less than ten minutes remaining but Hayden Hackney and Morgan Rogers scored late on to salvage a draw.

30TH JULY 1986

In financial peril and unable to pay outstanding moneys due to the Inland Revenue, Middlesbrough Football Club was ordered to be wound up by the High Court in London. The order was made on a petition by the Inland Revenue, claiming arrears of tax owed amounting to £115,156.

30TH JULY 2012

Doncaster Rovers' 24-year-old left-back George Friend completed a £100,000 move to Middlesbrough. During an eight-year stay on Teesside, Friend would become a fans' favourite, captain the club, win promotion and make 299 appearances for Boro.

31ST JULY 1986

Jack Charlton reacted to the news that Middlesbrough had been dealt a winding-up order by branding the plight of the club 'an absolute disgrace', adding, 'If the people and businessmen of Middlesbrough let the club die, they will regret it. A town without a football club is an anonymous place.' Meanwhile, a rescue act was forming behind the scenes to find a way to save the club.

MIDDLESBROUGH
On This Day

AUGUST

1st AUGUST 1995

Hundreds of fans queued outside Ayresome Park – some lining up overnight – to get their hands on the newly released Boro replica shirts as supporters got kitted out ahead of the club's return to Premier League football.

2nd AUGUST 1986

With the club on the brink of bankruptcy with unsustainable debts and struggling to pay players' wages, the Ayresome Park gates were padlocked as Middlesbrough Football Club looked to have come to a traumatic end.

3rd AUGUST 1976

Boro began their tour of Finland against Finnish top-flight table-toppers Kuopion Palloseura. Trailing 1-0, after the interval Jack Charlton changed things around and Boro went on to win 2-1 with goals from Phil Boersma and John Craggs.

4th AUGUST 2007

AZ Alkmaar provided the opposition for the final pre-season friendly as goals from Stewart Downing and Yakubu helped Boro see off the Dutch side with a 2-0 win at the Riverside.

5th AUGUST 1975

En route to Anglo-Scottish Cup glory, Boro's 4-1 win over Carlisle United at Ayresome Park made it two wins out of two in the competition with Alan Willey (two), John Hickton with a penalty, and Ian Bailey getting the home side's goals.

5th AUGUST 1978

Boro scored all four goals of the game in the first half as they hammered Inverness Clachacuddin in a pre-season friendly in Scotland. Graeme Hedley scored twice, with David Armstrong and Stan Cummins also getting among the goals.

5th AUGUST 2002

Middlesbrough once again turned their transfer attention to Villa Park, this time to sign Aston Villa's Dutch midfielder George Boateng in a £5m deal. The capture of Boateng proved to be one of the most significant signings in the club's history, with the former Coventry City man instrumental in Boro's golden era that brought League Cup success and a place in the UEFA Cup Final.

6TH AUGUST 2002

Brazilian World Cup winner Juninho returned to Boro for a third spell as hundreds of supporters greeted the 'Little Fella' outside the Riverside. After putting pen to paper on a four-year deal, the £3.8m new signing pledged to bring the elusive first piece of major silverware to Teesside.

7TH AUGUST 1976

Graeme Hedley, 19, made an impressive debut in an Anglo-Scottish Cup tie against Hull City and was involved in both of Boro's goals in a 2-0 win. Wantaway midfielder Graeme Souness gave the holders the lead in the 64th minute before Phil Boersma doubled it six minutes later.

7TH AUGUST 1990

The *Evening Gazette* and Middlesbrough FC announced a new shirt sponsorship deal that saw the local newspaper's name feature on the front of the club's new home and away shirts.

8TH AUGUST 1995

Middlesbrough smashed their transfer record with the £5.25m capture of England international Nick Barmby from Tottenham Hotspur. The *Evening Gazette* reported how the lure of Bryan Robson had helped attract the new man to the club.

8TH AUGUST 1996

Boro took on Champions League winners Juventus at Cesena's Stadio Dino Manuzzi in a glamorous pre-season friendly. Fabrizio Ravanelli faced his former side who included new signings Zinedine Zidane, Alen Bokšić and Christian Vieri in their line-up. Juventus led at half-time through a Vieri goal. The Bianconeri doubled their advantage when Alessandro Del Piero's long-range effort eluded the dive of Alan Miller. The game finished 2-1 after Nigel Pearson's header reduced the deficit with five minutes remaining.

9TH AUGUST 2015

Stewart Downing made his first appearance since completing his £5m return from West Ham as Boro opened the season with a goalless encounter at Deepdale against newly promoted Preston North End.

BORO SMASHED THEIR TRANSFER RECORD WHEN SIGNING NICK BARMBY, SEEN HERE IN ACTION DURING THE 1995/96 SEASON (THE GAZETTE)

10TH AUGUST 1971

Boro completed their preparations for the new campaign as they entertained Portuguese giants Benfica at Ayresome Park. The match pitted two stars of the 1966 World Cup against each other as England hero Nobby Stiles turned out for Boro and Benfica boasted Eusébio – the 1966 tournament's top scorer – among their ranks. The home side opened the scoring through one of Middlesbrough's greatest goalscorers of all time as John Hickton headed home Johnny Vincent's free kick. Benfica equalised after 27 minutes when Eusébio – widely regarded as one of the greatest players ever – stabbed home a loose ball in the box.

11TH AUGUST 1976

Graeme Hedley was the architect in Boro's 1-0 victory at Sheffield United in the Anglo-Scottish Cup, making the winning goal for Graeme Souness to score his second of the tournament.

11TH AUGUST 1996

Inter Milan were the visitors for Willie Maddren's testimonial match. The Boro faithful turned out in their numbers to pay tribute to the former defender and manager, who had been diagnosed with motor neurone disease. New signing Emerson impressed as a sometimes bad-tempered affair ended goalless.

11TH AUGUST 2000

'Steve Snubs Boro' read the *Evening Gazette* back page after Bryan Robson had been thwarted in his attempt to bring Steve McManaman to Middlesbrough after the England international turned down a £9m move from Real Madrid.

12TH AUGUST 1972

Stan Anderson's side got off to a flying start to the season as youngster Malcolm Smith made his first league start and scored both of his side's goals as they fought back from a goal down to see off Sunderland.

13TH AUGUST 1994

The 'Robbo Revolution' kicked off against newly promoted Burnley in a First Division clash at a packed Ayresome Park, the last campaign at the famous ground. Boro made a promising start under new player-manager Bryan Robson with a 2-0 win courtesy of two first-half goals from John Hendrie. Alongside Robbo, the match brought full debuts for Alan Miller, the recent signing from Arsenal, £1m club record signing Neil Cox, Robson's former Manchester United team-mate Clayton Blackmore and ex-Sheffield Wednesday League Cup winner Nigel Pearson.

14TH AUGUST 1993

Making his first league start for the club, Alan Moore inspired Middlesbrough to a 3-2 win at Notts County on the opening day of the season. Continuing his excellent pre-season form, the Irish winger set up Paul Wilkinson to open the scoring after 19 minutes before doubling the lead with a shot from outside of the box. Three minutes after the break Moore scored his second goal with a stunning strike from outside the box that left Steve Cherry in the County goal rooted. Despite the Magpies' late fightback, Boro were always good value for the three points.

14TH AUGUST 2004

Newcastle United twice led at the Riverside but were pinned back twice in a Tees–Tyne derby draw in the opening game of the season. Craig Bellamy's first-half goal separated the sides until the 73rd minute when substitute Stewart Downing equalised. An Alan Shearer penalty had seemingly settled the clash in the visitors' favour with only seven minutes remaining until new signing Jimmy Floyd Hasselbaink scored a 90th-minute equaliser when he forced the ball home at the back post with a brave header.

15TH AUGUST 2023

Middlesbrough completed the signing of 24-year-old left-back Lukas Engel from Danish Superliga side Silkeborg on a four-year deal to become Michael Carrick's eighth senior signing of the summer.

16TH AUGUST 2008

Gareth Southgate's side got the season off to a flying start against Tottenham Hotspur. However, the deadlock was not broken until the 71st minute when David Wheater put Boro ahead. With four minutes to go ex-Spurs man Mido doubled the advantage and despite the visitors pulling one goal back from a Robert Huth own goal, Boro held on for the win.

17TH AUGUST 1974

Jack Charlton's newly promoted Boro produced an outstanding performance in the club's first top-flight fixture since 1954 as they hammered Birmingham City 3-0 at St Andrew's. The scoreline flattered the Blues as the visitors were dominant throughout. Charlton's men opened the scoring after 13 minutes when Willie Maddren ran through midfield, beat three opponents and put in a great cross for John Hickton to head home. Hickton almost doubled the lead when he hit the post, before Alan Foggon slammed home a loose ball in the penalty area after 25th minutes. A minute after the interval Bobby Murdoch, John Craggs and David Mills combined to set up Foggon for his second to complete the scoring.

17TH AUGUST 1996

Fabrizio Ravanelli scored a memorable hat-trick on his debut in a thrilling opening-day draw with Liverpool at a sold-out Riverside Stadium. Boro trailed to an early Stig Inge Bjørnebye goal before the Italian international equalised from the penalty spot to get off the mark for his new club. John Barnes restored the visitors' lead in a frantic opening half an hour before Ravanelli grabbed his second goal from close range to level matters at half-time. Boro's defence leaked a third goal as Robbie Fowler once again restored the Merseysiders' lead after 65 minutes but with just nine minutes remaining, new fans' favourite Ravanelli slotted home his third goal after wrong-footing David James to make it 3-3 and cap off one of the most remarkable starts to the season witnessed on Teesside.

18TH AUGUST 1979

After a first-half stalemate, Boro led six minutes after the interval at White Hart Lane when David Armstrong burst into the box and fired the ball past Barry Daines. Boro doubled their advantage through Micky Burns after good work from David Hodgson, David Armstrong and Boško Janković. In the 70th minute Janković put the game beyond doubt when scoring Boro's third, beating three men then hammering the ball past the Spurs keeper. Spurs pulled a goal back in the 75th minute. Jim Platt was called into action to keep the score at 3-1 and in the final minute, John Craggs was carried off on a stretcher.

19TH AUGUST 2006

Gareth Southgate's first league match as Boro boss ended in frustration against newly promoted Reading at the Madejski Stadium as they squandered a two-goal lead to lose 3-2. Stewart Downing and Yakubu gave Boro a healthy cushion after just 21 minutes but the lead was wiped out late in the first half. Future Boro striker Leroy Lita grabbed the winner in the second period and the visitors also had a Mark Viduka goal ruled out for offside.

20TH AUGUST 1995

New signing Nick Barmby outshone Arsenal debutants Dennis Bergkamp and David Platt at Highbury as the former Tottenham Hotspur man made his debut in Boro's first match back in the Premier League. The England forward fired Boro into the lead just after the hour mark to stun the Gunners' new manager, former Boro gaffer Bruce Rioch. Ian Wright headed home the Londoners' equaliser before half-time and despite a second-half onslaught, the score remained 1-1 as Boro held on for a point in front of the Sky Sports *Super Sunday* cameras.

21ST AUGUST 1993

Alan Kernaghan scored his final goal for the club in Boro's first home match back in the First Division, with Paul Wilkinson and John Hendrie getting on the scoresheet in a 3-0 victory over Derby County to keep Boro on track for their best start to a season in 68 years.

21ST AUGUST 2003

Spanish international midfielder Gaizka Mendieta signed for Middlesbrough on loan from Lazio as the 'ideal player', according to boss Steve McClaren, to replace Geremi who had excelled as a loan star in the previous campaign.

22ND AUGUST 1986

Boro were saved at the 11th hour after a consortium that had come together to work out a way for the football club – albeit as the new company, Middlesbrough Football & Athletic Company (1986) Limited – to survive. The long-running battle brought together local and national stakeholders including ICI, Scottish and Newcastle Breweries, Steve Gibson and Henry Moszkowicz, who had battled to ensure the club survived. In London, notes from representatives of the club's legal advisors and the Football League were passed between each other in separate rooms as Boro edged perilously close to extinction. If all the documents were not completed and a package to save the club was not agreed by 5.30pm, the Football League stated that they would announce that the fixture list for Middlesbrough for the following season – scheduled to kick off the next day – would be null and void. With ten minutes to spare, an agreement had been reached with the Football League and the club had been saved, with Steve Gibson later praising the important role of ICI's Colin Henderson in securing a bond from the firm whereby ICI would pick up a major part of any subsequent debt and would pay a substantial amount first. A press conference was convened at Middlesbrough Town Hall and Colin Henderson and Steve Gibson announced that Middlesbrough had been saved and that they would play their league game with Port Vale, scheduled for the next day, at Hartlepool United's Victoria Ground while arrangements were made to prepare Ayresome Park for football once again.

22ND AUGUST 1992

Leeds United arrived at Ayresome Park as First Division champions for the all-ticket Premier League clash. Within nine minutes Boro were 2-0 up courtesy of a brace by Paul Wilkinson, assisted on each occasion by former Elland Road winger Tommy Wright. After the interval it was Wright who added to Boro's tally with a header past John Lukic before former Whites attacker John Hendrie ran on to a Wright pass before cutting inside to fire in the Teessiders' fourth. The visitors responded through a goal from French maverick Eric Cantona but it proved a mere consolation for the West Yorkshire side.

23RD AUGUST 1958

Boro recorded their highest ever league win as they opened their campaign with a stunning 9-0 victory over Brighton & Hove Albion at Ayresome Park. New captain Brian Clough scored five of the goals while Bill Harris and Alan Peacock each grabbed braces in what proved to be a baptism of fire for the south coast side and goalkeeper David Hollins after their promotion from the Third Division North. According to the *Evening Gazette* match report, 'At the end of a nightmare match for young Hollins, Clough went up to the young keeper and offered his sincere sympathy.'

23RD AUGUST 1986

Following the last-minute reprieve from extinction the previous day, Middlesbrough Football & Athletic Club (1892) Ltd was no more and Middlesbrough Football & Athletic Company (1986) Ltd played their first professional match against Port Vale at Hartlepool United's Victoria Ground with Ayresome Park not ready to host the games. It kicked off at 6.30pm as Hartlepool had played Cardiff City there earlier in the day. A crowd of 3,690 turned out for Boro's first match in the third tier since 1967 and Bruce Rioch's young guns – the team's average age was under 22 years old – made a storming start. A brace from Archie Stephens – one of the players who at one stage had looked set to leave on a free transfer with the club having entered voluntary liquidation – gave Boro a 2-0 half-time lead. Against the inexperienced side, Port Vale found a way back into the game and pulled a goal back through Richard O'Kelly before Paul Maguire equalised with just five minutes remaining.

FORMER ELLAND ROAD WINGER TOMMY WRIGHT WAS BOTH CREATOR AND SCORER IN BORO'S 4-1 WIN OVER CHAMPIONS LEEDS UNITED.

24TH AUGUST 2002

Debutant Massimo Maccarone's brace failed to inspire an opening-day Boro win at the Riverside against Fulham as the Cottagers struck in the 89th and 95th minutes to steal a draw and deny the £8.15m record signing a dream start despite a man-of-the-match display.

25TH AUGUST 1981

Dutch international midfielder Heini Otto completed a £125,000 move from FC Twente to Middlesbrough, scoring ten minutes into his debut four days later against FA Cup holders Spurs. Otto proved to be a fans' favourite at Ayresome Park during his time with the club before his departure to Den Haag in summer 1985.

26TH AUGUST 1995

A crowd of 28,286 packed into the Cellnet Riverside Stadium for Boro's first match at their new, state-of-the-art £16m home after construction workers, safety officials and club staff had worked round the clock to ensure the showpiece fixture against Chelsea went ahead. Impressive Boro broke the deadlock just before the break when Nick Barmby squared to Craig Hignett, who rifled the ball beyond Dmitri Kharine and into the top corner for the first goal at the stadium. In the second half Norwegian striker Jan Åge Fjørtoft added a second for Middlesbrough for his first goal of the season to make sure the home side began life on the banks of the River Tees with a win.

27TH AUGUST 1927

Middlesbrough's return to the top flight ended in a 3-0 defeat against Manchester United at Old Trafford, although the local press reported that the scoreline had flattered the home side.

28TH AUGUST 1993

A topsy-turvy match at Molineux saw Lennie Lawrence's in-form side continue their fantastic start to the season as they recorded a fourth successive win. John Hendrie put Boro a goal up after just three minutes but Wolves fought back to lead 2-1 at the break. Hendrie added his second with 17 minutes remaining and with just five minutes left, youngster Jamie Pollock fired in a speculative long-range effort that Mike Stowell could only parry into his own net.

29TH AUGUST 1959

After a draw and a loss in their opening fixtures, Boro produced a stunning away win as Alan Peacock scored four goals in a 7-1 win at Derby County's Baseball Ground as the Teessiders netted five times after the break. Billy Day, Bill Harris and Eddy Holliday scored Middlesbrough's other goals.

30TH AUGUST 1997

Robbie Mustoe and Mikkel Beck scored the goals as Andy Townsend, the new signing from Aston Villa, made his debut in a 2-0 win at Tranmere Rovers.

31ST AUGUST 1927

A midweek summer evening brought the return of top-flight football to Ayresome Park for the first time in three seasons with boss Peter McWilliam's former club Tottenham Hotspur the visitors as the home side ran out impressive 3-0 winners. So impressive was the performance that 'Old Bird', the local *Sports Gazette* reporter exclaimed, 'a more glorious display of real football has never been witnessed at Ayresome Park than that of Wednesday'. John McKay grabbed the opening goal from close range after 35 minutes, prompting a 'deafening' roar from the terraces, and the lead was doubled midway through the second half courtesy of Owen Williams before Spurs grabbed a goal back from the spot. Boro cemented victory courtesy of a close-range George Camsell strike as the man who scored a record 59 league goals in the previous season's promotion campaign proved he could score goals at the highest level.

31ST AUGUST 2009

The *Evening Gazette* reported that Boro's record signing Afonso Alves was set to seal a cut-price switch to Qatari club Al Sadd after the Brazilian had failed to impress on Teesside. Despite a significant financial loss, the money saved on wages was welcomed and the deal was completed the following week.

MIDDLESBROUGH
On This Day

SEPTEMBER

1ST SEPTEMBER 1903

The football fanatics of Teesside were afforded their first glimpse of Middlesbrough's new Ayresome Park ground with Glasgow Celtic the visitors for a friendly. A crowd of 7,000 turned out for the prestigious fixture, with the home side recording a 1-0 win courtesy of a goal by Willie White.

2ND SEPTEMBER 1895

Attempting to boost support for the football club, the Middlesbrough directors resolved that a circular be drawn up and issued to the gentlemen of the town, calling attention to the trophies held by the teams, the club's amateur status and asking for support with application forms for memberships included.

2ND SEPTEMBER 1986

Middlesbrough played their first match back at Ayresome Park since the gates of the ground had reopened. Fittingly the first visitors were Hartlepool United, the club that had come to Boro's aid to host their opening league clash with Port Vale. The League Cup tie brought a 2-0 win for the home side courtesy of goals from Stuart Ripley and Gary Hamilton in front of 7,735 fans – the club's biggest home crowd in the competition since 10,389 turned out for an October 1982 exit to Burnley.

3RD SEPTEMBER 1927

Middlesbrough recorded a 4-2 win over Everton at Ayresome Park on a day when the pre-match focus was on George Camsell and Dixie Dean – two of the game's great goalscorers – leading the line for their respective clubs. In this instance it was Camsell who came out on top as his four goals helped his side to a second successive win, although Dean did manage one goal.

3RD SEPTEMBER 1938

Wilf Mannion, Micky Fenton and Benny Yorston were the goal heroes as Wilf Gillow's side left Stoke City's Victoria Ground with a 3-1 win. The win put Boro in second place in the top flight as police had to clear home fans who held a demonstration aimed at management and directors for the lack of transfer activity.

3RD SEPTEMBER 1977

Boro legend Willie Maddren made his final appearance for the club while record £135,000 signing Billy Ashcroft made his debut having completed his move from Wrexham in midweek. However, it was Cyrille Regis – making his West Brom league debut – who grabbed the headlines at The Hawthorns as he doubled his side's lead on 20 minutes just five minutes after future Ayresome Park gaffer Bryan Robson had given the Throstles the lead. David Mills – who himself would go on to become West Brom's record signing – pulled a goal back for Middlesbrough but the home side held on.

3RD SEPTEMBER 1983

A 2-2 draw with Leeds United in Boro's first home game of the season was overshadowed by widespread hooliganism by visiting supporters on a weekend to forget as trouble erupted at several grounds across the country. In the aftermath of the violence, it was reported in the press that Boro could consider banning Leeds United supporters from Ayresome Park for good after 200 seats were ripped out by travelling fans and a toilet block damaged. Middlesbrough chairman Mike McCulloch raised the issue of compensation with the FA, and the club estimated lost revenue of around £20,000 owing to fans staying away in anticipation of trouble.

4TH SEPTEMBER 1899

Grove Hill's Robert Page made history in the third game of the club's first season in the Football League as he notched Boro's first league goal, in a 3-1 loss at Burslem Port Vale.

5TH SEPTEMBER 1959

After a goalless first half against Plymouth Argyle at Ayresome Park, Brian Clough – described in the *Sunday Mirror* match report as 'the man who has been passed over by the England selectors more times than a hen egg in a turkey house' – scored four goals and Alan Peacock a brace in a 6-2 win.

6TH SEPTEMBER 1983

An entertaining Tees–Tyne derby at Ayresome Park ended in dramatic fashion as Malcolm Allison's side made it seven points from their three opening games of the season courtesy of a 3-2 win. Dave Currie gave Boro a half-time lead before Kevin Keegan equalised for Newcastle United. Currie scored again but, to quote Newcastle newspaper *The Journal*, 'It seemed that former Boro player David Mills had made a timely return to rescue United from a bad taste of Currie,' as he scored an equaliser. However, rather than a former Boro boy stealing the headlines, it was teenager Gary Hamilton who proved to be the match-winner as he smashed the ball in with just four minutes remaining.

6TH SEPTEMBER 2000

Bryan Robson's side surrendered a three-goal lead with less than 30 minutes remaining as Derby County fought back at Pride Park for a 3-3 draw. Boro appeared to be cruising to a second Premier League win of the campaign courtesy of goals from Alen Bokšić, Joseph-Désiré Job and Brian Deane. Former Boro coach Jim Smith's substitutions proved inspired as substitutes Malcolm Christie and Georgi Kinkladze transformed the match, with Christie scoring two goals either side of a Branko Strupar goal.

7TH SEPTEMBER 1946

Boro hosted Stoke City in their first home game of the season and were in confident mood after wins at Aston Villa and Liverpool. The police had ordered the gates of Ayresome Park to be closed as they estimated some 46,000 (compared to an official attendance of 43,685) had descended on the ground in eager anticipation of another Middlesbrough win. However, few could have expected what was to follow in one of the most incredible matches ever witnessed at Ayresome Park. The sides went in at half-time level at 3-3, with Micky Fenton scoring all of the home side's goals. Into the second half, Wilf Mannion restored the lead before Freddie Steele completed a hat-trick of his own to level for the Potters. It was not until the dying minutes that Fenton scored his fourth and Boro's fifth to record a third successive victory. Following the match, so impressed were the visitors by Mannion that Stoke City manager Bob McGrory announced that the Potteries club had tabled an offer for the 'Golden Boy'.

8TH SEPTEMBER 1973

'Big Mal' Allison's Crystal Palace were outdone by 'Big Jack' Charlton's Boro as John Hickton, Brian Taylor and David Mills scored for the visitors in a 3-2 win that proved to be the beginning of a 24-game unbeaten run in the Second Division.

8TH SEPTEMBER 1982

Tony Mowbray was handed the number seven shirt as he faced a baptism of fire on his Boro debut away at a star-studded Newcastle United with the unenviable task of marking Kevin Keegan. Relegated the previous season, Boro were pointless and had shipped seven goals in their opening two matches. Paul Ward also made his bow and Bobby Murdoch's debutants helped arrest the rot as his side battled back after falling behind to a second-half Mick Channon goal to draw thanks to a Darren Wood equaliser.

9TH SEPTEMBER 1899

Small Heath were the visitors to the Linthorpe Road Ground for Boro's first home game as a league club. The Midlands side's 3-1 win underlined the task Middlesbrough – who had lost both of their matches to date – faced in adapting to league football. Bob McRoberts scored a hat-trick for the visitors with Michael Murphy scoring for the home side.

9TH SEPTEMBER 1935

George Camsell scored five in a 7-2 win at Villa Park to make it 12 goals in two away games for the Teessiders as they went top of the First Division. The *Birmingham Gazette* described Villa's heaviest home league defeat since the First World War as 'their severest football lesson for years'.

10TH SEPTEMBER 2002

Szilárd Németh (two) and Massimo Maccarone scored the goals as Middlesbrough triumphed in the Tees–Wear derby at the Riverside Stadium to go fourth in the Premier League.

11TH SEPTEMBER 1965

Bryan 'Taffy' Orritt – the versatile forward who played in defence, midfield, attack and even as a goalkeeper – fittingly also had the honour of becoming the club's first ever substitute when he replaced the injured Nev Chapman at Preston. Since the beginning of the season clubs had been allowed to name a substitute who was permitted to replace a team-mate – in theory – only in instances of injury.

11TH SEPTEMBER 1994

The final Tees–Wear derby at Ayresome Park ended in a 2-2 draw live on Tyne Tees Television. Ahead of kick-off, new boy Jaime Moreno was presented to the home fans. The Bolivian international could only look on as his new team-mates trailed 2-0 with just 11 minutes left on the clock before Alan Moore pulled a goal back and Nigel Pearson equalised with a close-range header in the 81st minute.

11TH SEPTEMBER 2001

A low crowd turned out at the Riverside as David Murphy, Szilárd Németh and Mark Wilson all made goalscoring full debuts in the 3-1 League Cup second round win over Northampton Town. The match attracted a ground record low attendance of 3,918 as many supporters stayed away as the tragedy of the 9/11 attacks in the US unfolded on television.

12TH SEPTEMBER 1903

James Clifton Robinson, president and managing director of Imperial Tramways and a shareholder at the club, performed the official opening ceremony of Ayresome Park with a golden key as a crowd of 30,000 packed into Middlesbrough's new home. The ground, designed by Archibald Leitch, featured a new main stand with the opposite stand relocated from the club's former home at the Linthorpe Road Ground. Sunderland were the visitors for the first home league game of the season as Boro looked to record their first win after losing their opening away fixture at Sheffield Wednesday. Just before half-time, Scotsman Joe Cassidy made sure of his place in the history books by scoring the first goal at Ayresome Park to give Boro the lead. The Wearsiders levelled after half-time but Boro hit back in less than a minute through Alex Brown. Unfortunately, Sunderland went on to win 3-2 to put a dampener on Boro's big day.

13TH SEPTEMBER 1988

Youngster Colin Cooper's impressive performances for Bruce Rioch's Boro earned him an England under-21 cap against Denmark at Watford's Vicarage Road in a goalless draw.

13TH SEPTEMBER 1998

Hámilton Ricard smashed a double as newly promoted Boro stunned caretaker manager David Pleat's Tottenham Hotspur at White Hart Lane in front of the national TV cameras. Vladimír Kinder, a late substitute for Paul Gascoigne who received a warm ovation from the home fans, scored a long-range effort to make it 3-0 shortly before the end.

ACTION FROM THE OPENING LEAGUE FIXTURE AT MIDDLESBROUGH'S NEW AYRESOME PARK GROUND (HARRY GREENMON)

14TH SEPTEMBER 1985

Sunderland legend and former Canaries forward Gary Rowell scored the fastest penalty in Boro's history to give the home side the lead after just 38 seconds in a 1-1 draw against his old club Norwich City.

14TH SEPTEMBER 1991

Boro recorded a 3-0 victory over Leicester City in front of 16,673 at Ayresome Park. Bernie Slaven's fourth goal of the season and a brace from new marksman Paul Wilkinson extended the team's winning run to five in a row.

15TH SEPTEMBER 1894

Bishop Auckland were the visitors to the Linthorpe Road Ground as Middlesbrough kicked off their defence of the Northern League title with a 2-2 draw. There was little doubt who the man of the match was, with the performance of Strophair in the visitors' goal described in the following Monday's *North Eastern Daily Gazette* as 'the finest exhibition of custodianship witnessed in Middlesbrough for many a long day ... the Auckland man's play was at times little short of marvellous, and fairly roused the feelings of those present, ringing cheers greeting him'.

16TH SEPTEMBER 1899

At the fourth time of asking, the Football League new boys got a point on the board as they faced New Brighton Tower in front of 2,000 spectators. Robert Eglington scored on his league debut on the cusp of half-time to pull Boro level after Tommy Leigh had put the Tower ahead.

16TH SEPTEMBER 2004

Boro's first venture into major European competition brought Baník Ostrava to the Riverside for the first of a UEFA Cup group stage qualifying double-header against the Slovakians. With visiting goalkeeper Martin Raška's saves having frustrated the majority of the 29,746 throughout the first half, it was not until the 57th minute that the Teessiders finally broke the deadlock. The historic goal came from recent signing Jimmy Floyd Hasselbaink, with fellow new acquisition Mark Viduka adding a second within six minutes. With ten minutes remaining the Australian international added his second goal with a guided header that put Boro in the driving seat heading to the Czech Republic's former 'Steel Heart'. The historic Boro line-up was: Mark Schwarzer, Stuart Parnaby, Frank Queudrue, Chris Riggott, Gareth Southgate, George Boateng, Ray Parlour, Szilárd Németh, Mark Viduka, Jimmy Floyd Hasselbaink, Bolo Zenden. Subs: Carlo Nash, Colin Cooper, Doriva, James Morrison, Stewart Downing, Joseph-Désiré Job.

17TH **SEPTEMBER 1973**

Lisbon Lion Bobby Murdoch completed his move from Glasgow Celtic to Middlesbrough after Jack Charlton acted on a phone call from his close friend Jock Stein in which the Scottish club's manager explained he was giving Murdoch a free transfer. Charlton told the *Evening Gazette's* Cliff Mitchell, 'I asked if I could have a word with him [Murdoch] before anybody else ... Jock replied that he was going to tell our kid at Preston [Bobby Charlton was manager at Deepdale] about Bobby, but that he was telling me first ... I am as chuffed as little apples that he's going to give us control in the middle of the field, where I need it most. I've been an admirer of Bobby for a long time – ever since he whacked one past me in the European Cup semi-final between Celtic and Leeds in 1970.' The Scottish international travelled to Brisbane Road with his new team-mates but was on the sidelines to witness the goalless draw.

18TH **SEPTEMBER 1996**

Four goals from Fabrizio Ravanelli helped Boro to a 7-0 League Cup second round first leg win over Hereford United at the Riverside Stadium. Emerson, Branco and Republic of Ireland international Curtis Fleming scored the other goals in the club-record League Cup victory.

19TH **SEPTEMBER 1959**

Brian Clough took his goal tally to nine for the season as his second hat-trick of the campaign handed in-form Boro a 3-0 win over Charlton Athletic at Ayresome Park that lifted the Teessiders to second place in the Second Division.

19TH **SEPTEMBER 1973**

The Ayresome Park North Midland League match against Halifax Town was the unlikely stage for two of the most decorated players in British football to make their Boro bows. World Cup winner Jack Charlton – readying himself to take part in Eusébio's testimonial in Lisbon the following week – and Lisbon Lion Bobby Murdoch made their debuts for Boro's reserves. Some 2,000 fans turned out for the second-string match, which finished 1-1, and it was Charlton who headed the home side into the lead before Willie Irvine scored a late equaliser for the visitors.

20TH SEPTEMBER 1948

Tom Blenkinsop played for the English league against the Irish league in a 5-1 win for the home side at Anfield. The Boro defender was a late call-up after Blackpool's Harry Johnston, pencilled in to captain the side, reported unfit.

21ST SEPTEMBER 1974

It was fourth time lucky for Jack Charlton's men at Ayresome Park as they finally recorded a home win in their first season back in the First Division as they overcame Manchester City 3-0. David Mills scored a first-half opener and Alan Foggon netted a late brace. Alan Willey made his debut for the home side and City's Scottish international Willie Donachie saw red for punching Foggon in a clash with the two-goal hero.

21ST SEPTEMBER 1993

Craig Hignett became the last player to score four goals in a match at Ayresome Park as Boro swept aside Brighton & Hove Albion with a 5-0 League Cup second round first leg win. All of the ex-Crewe man's goals arrived in the first half, before John Hendrie added a fifth in the 52nd minute.

22ND SEPTEMBER 1973

Boro fans were joined by a contingent of Glasgow Celtic fans at Blackpool's Bloomfield Road as Bobby Murdoch made his league debut for Jack Charlton's team, replacing the injured Eric McMordie. The goalless draw coupled with a scoreless clash at Ayresome Park meant the Seasiders were the only team Boro failed to score against in the Second Division that season.

23RD SEPTEMBER 1899

At the fifth time of asking, Middlesbrough finally triumphed in the Football League with a 1-0 win over Grimsby Town at the Linthorpe Road Ground, and with it recorded the club's first clean sheet in the competition. Robert Eglinton scored the only goal of the game to the delight of the majority of the 4,000 crowd.

24TH SEPTEMBER 1966

A penalty king is born! John Hickton, Middlesbrough's new signing from Sheffield Wednesday, made a goalscoring debut on his 22nd birthday in a Third Division clash with Workington Town. Having been convinced to sign for the Teessiders after club secretary Harry Green drove to Hickton's home in Chesterfield to complete the deal, early in the game he must have questioned his decision as Workington raced into a two-goal lead. Wearing the number five shirt and playing at centre-half, the new man struggled to contain Max Tolson, who scored both of the visitors' goals. However, Boro and Hickton enjoyed a change in fortune when on 37 minutes they were awarded a penalty. In the absence of Boro's regular penalty taker Dickie Rooks – for whom 'Big John' was deputising at centre-half – Hickton stepped up and smashed the ball into the net to bring the home side back into the game. After the break, Arthur Horsfield scored a brace for the second match running to help the Teessiders to a 3-2 win, their first home victory of the campaign, and with it two vital points.

24TH SEPTEMBER 1974

With Boro leading 1-0 through a Graeme Souness goal, the home match with Leicester City was abandoned after 29 minutes due to floodlight failure. Not to be denied, the rescheduled fixture in December brought a 3-0 Middlesbrough win courtesy of goals from Alan Foggon (two) and Alan Willey, later an inductee into the National Soccer Hall of Fame for his goalscoring exploits with Minnesota Kicks in the USA.

24TH SEPTEMBER 1994

A solitary John Hendrie strike against Bristol City at Ashton Gate ensured all three points headed back to Teesside to get Boro back to winning ways in the First Division after a first defeat at Vale Park the previous weekend.

25TH SEPTEMBER 1997

The Mirror reported that new man Paul Merson was facing travel torment as he commuted from Hertfordshire to Teesside. Despite Merson having stated that he was determined to make a go of it at Middlesbrough, Tottenham and West Ham were said to be monitoring the situation should the former Arsenal man be interested in a return to London.

26TH SEPTEMBER 1970

John Hickton scored his fourth Boro hat-trick after the Teessiders recovered from falling two goals behind to QPR to win 6-2. Hughie McIllmoyle (two) and Derrick Downing scored the home side's other goals.

27TH SEPTEMBER 1994

Paul Wilkinson, wearing the captain's armband for the night, ended his barren run in front of goal with his first Boro hat-trick as Middlesbrough cruised past Scarborough 4-1 on the night (8-2 aggregate) to reach the third round of the League Cup. The visitors opened the scoring at Ayresome Park from the penalty spot before Wilkinson equalised to level the score on the night going into the interval. In the second half Wilkinson added two further goals to his tally before Craig Hignett completed the scoring in the final League Cup match to be held at Ayresome Park.

28TH SEPTEMBER 1946

Despite having appeared for England in wartime internationals, owing to the Second World War George Hardwick and Wilf Mannion had to wait until 1946 for their full international debuts at the age of 26 and 28 respectively. The clash against Northern Ireland in Belfast saw Hardwick captain the team to a 7-2 win as Mannion made up for lost time and scored England's second, third and fifth goals.

28TH SEPTEMBER 1991

The fastest derby goal at Ayresome Park was scored after only 17 seconds by Bernie Slaven for his fifth goal of the season in a 2-1 win. The Republic of Ireland international's goal arrived after a stray Kevin Ball back-pass caught the visiting Sunderland goalkeeper off guard and he could only palm the ball into the path of Slaven, who tapped home in front of a jubilant Holgate End. Boro doubled their lead through Paul Wilkinson ahead of half-time and looked to be cruising until John Hendrie and Sunderland left-back Paul Hardyman were dismissed following a tussle. The visitors benefited more from the dismissals and pulled a goal back through Kieron Brady but Boro held on.

29TH SEPTEMBER 1926

George Camsell scored the only goal at Bradford City in Boro's fourth successive win since the ex-miner replaced the injured Jimmy McClelland in the side.

30TH SEPTEMBER 1950

Wilf Mannion scored a first-half hat-trick and Alex McCrae a second-half treble as the Teessiders climbed to second in the First Division following a stunning 8-0 win over Huddersfield Town at Ayresome Park. Johnny Spuhler and Bradfordian Geoff Walker scored the home side's other goals.

30TH SEPTEMBER 1995

Reigning Premier League champions Blackburn Rovers were defeated 2-0 in their first visit to the Riverside courtesy of goals from Nick Barmby and Craig Hignett, a pairing dubbed 'the midget gems'. The match is also remembered for an iconic moment between Jan Åge Fjørtoft and Tim Flowers when the pair shared a kiss after the Norwegian international attempted to block the England goalkeeper from releasing the ball for a counter-attack.

30TH SEPTEMBER 2004

Boro youth product James Morrison made history as he scored the club's first away goal in major European competition as the Teessiders, leading 3-0 from the first leg, completed the job against Baník Ostrava to progress to the UEFA Cup group stage. Several of Steve McClaren's key players were missing through injury and the home side took advantage through a spectacular long-range volley by David Bystroň. When Franck Queudrue was dismissed for a second bookable offence with just over 30 minutes remaining, Boro survived an Ostrava onslaught and in the final minute Morrison ran on to a George Boateng pass and slotted home coolly to make it 1-1 on the night and 4-1 on aggregate.

WILF MANNION NOTCHED A FIRST-HALF HAT-TRICK IN AN 8-0 ROUT OF HUDDERSFIELD TOWN AT AYRESOME PARK.

MIDDLESBROUGH
On This Day

OCTOBER

1ST OCTOBER 1988

Boro recorded their first away win since returning to the First Division as opposing Scottish strikers Bernie Slaven and David Speedie both scored hat-tricks. Slaven's three goals in a 4-3 win at Coventry City meant the former Albion Rovers man netted his first top-flight treble and the club's first in the top tier since James McCormack bagged a treble in a 7-1 win at Blackburn Rovers in 1947. Mark Burke scored Boro's other goal.

2ND OCTOBER 1973

In front of 22,184, the biggest attendance of the season to date, Boro moved clear at the top of the Second Division with 3-2 win over Leyton Orient. Alan Foggon put Boro ahead and John Hickton doubled the lead with 14 minutes remaining with a hotly disputed penalty. But they almost threw away two precious points as they conceded twice in three minutes and the Londoners looked like they had grabbed an unlikely draw. With just six minutes remaining, however, substitute Harry Charlton's cross was met by John Hickton, who headed home the final goal of the game.

3RD OCTOBER 1960

Gordon Jones made his debut, Brian Clough scored a brace and Alan Peacock added another in Boro's first League Cup match. Unfortunately, visitors Cardiff City scored four times in the seven-goal thriller to condemn the home side to defeat in front of 15,695 at Ayresome Park. To Boro's credit, they battled hard as for nearly an hour the South Wales side had a numerical advantage after Eddy Holliday was carried off after only 32 minutes in the days before substitutions.

3RD OCTOBER 1998

Paul Gascoigne scored a 90th-minute free kick to top off a fantastic performance in a 4-0 win over Danny Wilson's hapless Sheffield Wednesday as Bryan Robson's men recorded their first league home win of the season. Mikkel Beck's brace had given the home side a commanding half-time lead and within four minutes of the restart Hámilton Ricard added his eighth goal of the campaign.

4TH OCTOBER 1890

Boro recorded their biggest winning margin as they hammered visitors Scarborough 11-0 in an FA Cup qualifying round tie at the Linthorpe Road Ground. The cup clash attracted a crowd of around 2,000 and according to the *York Herald*, 'Middlesbrough appeared for the first time in their new colours, dark blue jerseys, which showed up in strong contrast to the white colours of the visitors.'

4TH OCTOBER 1980

Only 12,958 fans – the lowest attendance of the season – witnessed Boro's biggest home win in nearly two years as they went goal crazy against Norwich City at Ayresome Park. Tony McAndrew headed the opening goal on his 200th league appearance after the Norwich goalkeeper Roger Hansbury could only parry David Armstrong's effort. After spurning several chances, Boško Janković added a second goal after half an hour when Hansbury failed to deal with a cross. Into the second half, a miserable day for Hansbury was compounded as he leaked a further four goals, beginning with Armstrong's floated corner that appeared to go into the net without anyone touching the ball. More chaos in the Canaries' defence saw Clive Woods deflect the ball into his own net and despite a Justin Fashanu goal for the visitors, Boro soon restored their four-goal cushion after Craig Johnston headed home an Armstrong corner. The final goal of the game came with 80 minutes on the clock when Janković ran through to score his second of the 6-1 win.

5TH OCTOBER 1946

High-flying Boro, having won four of their opening six matches, welcomed Chelsea to Ayresome Park as George Hardwick and Wilf Mannion returned to the side after missing the loss at Sheffield United owing to international duty. The 'Golden Boy' made an immediate impact, scoring a brace after one-time England international Micky Fenton had given the home side a 1-0 half-time lead.

6TH OCTOBER 1996

In the wake of a 4-0 loss at Southampton in Boro's last Premier League outing, Bryan Robson was linked with a double raid on Blackburn Rovers. The *Sunday Mirror* reported that Nick Barmby would be offered as 'the bait' in a bid to bring goalkeeper Tim Flowers and centre-back Colin Hendry to Teesside, who Robbo considered the ideal solution to his side's leaky defence.

7TH **OCTOBER 1905**

George Thomas Reid became the first Boro player to score a hat-trick at Ayresome Park as Bury were on the wrong end of a 5-1 hammering at the hands of Alex Mackie's side. World record signing Alf Common and Charles Hewitt completed the scoring for the home team.

7TH **OCTOBER 2023**

A goalless Tees–Wear derby was turned on its head on the stroke of half-time following Dan Neil's red card in first-half injury time. The floodgates opened after 58 minutes when Stadium of Light academy graduate Sam Greenwood put the visitors ahead. Matt Crooks doubled the lead two minutes later and Isaiah Jones made it three with 18 minutes remaining. Marcus Forss finished Sunderland off as he scored in the 90th minute long after thousands of the home support had departed.

8TH **OCTOBER 1973**

Top-flight Manchester United were dumped out of the League Cup at Old Trafford by second-tier high-flyers Boro. Within three minutes Ferryhill youngster Malcolm Smith – described in the *Manchester Evening News* as an 'unknown stand-in' – scored for the visitors and despite a frantic onslaught by the home side, an inspired defensive display ensured Jack Charlton's men progressed to the next round.

9TH **OCTOBER 1976**

We are top of the league! Boro occupied top spot in the First Division for the first time since December 1950 as Graeme Souness scored the only goal of the game against Norwich City. However, Jack Charlton's team left it late with the Scot's strike coming with just seven minutes left in a match that, according to newspaper reports, could have easily finished 5-4 such was the glut of chances missed. Making the most of the moment, supporters in the Holgate waited behind after the final whistle and remained until their heroes returned to the pitch.

10TH **OCTOBER 1987**

Bernie Slaven scored his first league hat-trick for Boro as struggling Huddersfield Town were hammered 4-1 at Leeds Road. Brian Laws scored the visitors' other goal as he returned to haunt his old club.

MATT CROOKS WAS AMONGST THE GOALS AS BORO RAN RIOT AT THE STADIUM OF LIGHT IN A FAMOUS 4-0 WIN.

11TH OCTOBER 1995

Middlesbrough stars Nick Barmby and Jan Åge Fjørtoft faced off at international level as England and Norway laboured to a drab 0-0 draw in a friendly match in Oslo.

12TH OCTOBER 1995

With rumours that Terry Venables would depart his role as England boss after Euro '96, Bryan Robson as second-favourite with the bookmakers to succeed 'El Tel'. Newcastle manager Kevin Keegan was installed as evens favourite, with Robson available at 9/4 with William Hill. Incidentally, eventual successor Glenn Hoddle was priced at 12/1 and former Boro boss Jack Charlton was a 16/1 outsider.

13TH OCTOBER 1999

Juninho scored his first goal since returning to the club on loan from Atlético Madrid as the Brazilian's strike proved the difference between Boro and Watford in a League Cup third round clash at the Riverside in front of a ground record low attendance of 8,843.

14TH OCTOBER 1996

The last Wear–Tees derby at Roker Park produced an entertaining 2-2 draw as Boro twice squandered the lead in front of the Sky cameras. Emerson opened the scoring with a first-half deflected thunderbolt that left Tony Coton grasping at thin air before Alex Rae levelled from the spot after Phil Whelan had committed a foul in the area. Fabrizio Ravanelli restored the lead with a close-range finish but Craig Russell equalised eight minutes later.

15TH OCTOBER 1997

Local lad Andy Campbell and Scouse schemer Craig Hignett were the second-half goal heroes as Sunderland were dumped out of the League Cup in front of 26,451 at the Riverside Stadium.

16TH OCTOBER 1957

The beginning of the floodlight era at Ayresome Park was marked by the first of several floodlit friendlies. Arthur Fitzsimmons and Brian Clough scored the goals in a 2-0 win over Sunderland in front of 27,273 fans. The match is best remembered, however, for a goal that was not. Despite Lindy Delapenha – the first Jamaican to play in the Football League – seemingly having smashed his spot-kick into the back of the net, the ball slipped through – or put a hole in – the net and the referee awarded a goal kick to the Mackems.

OUR PIN-UP

'LINDY' DELAPENHA
Middlesbrough

16TH OCTOBER 1998

Boro snapped up former England international Brian Deane from Graeme Souness's Benfica in a £3m deal as the former Sheffield United marksman – the scorer of the Premier League's first goal – ended a brief stay in Portugal.

17TH OCTOBER 1993

Sunday afternoon football in front of a sparse crowd of 12,722 brought an impressive derby win over Terry Butcher's struggling Sunderland side. Boro showed their superiority after eight minutes when Craig Hignett put Boro ahead, before Don Goodman briefly fired the visitors level. Within ten minutes John Hendrie had restored the lead and Paul Wilkinson added a third with an effort that darted into the corner of Alec Chamberlain's net. A bad day for Sunderland got worse as Don Goodman skied a penalty before Wilko completed the rout with a flying back-post header from a Hendrie cross as Lennie Lawrence's men recorded their biggest league win over their Wearside rivals since 1936.

17TH OCTOBER 1995

Boro unveiled their new £4.75m Brazilian Footballer of the Year Juninho at the Riverside. The fee was the second largest paid in the club's history, £500,000 less than the £5.25m paid for Nick Barmby just two months earlier. The capture of the 'Little Fella' was the culmination of months of hard work by chief executive Keith Lamb and boss Bryan Robson, who had flown to Brazil to seal the deal. The world's football media turned up alongside thousands of ecstatic supporters – including many kids absent from school – as Juninho showed off a glimpse of his skills on the pitch alongside Robson. Local news reporter Ian Payne captured the sense of occasion, 'It's the half-term holidays next week, but looking around you'd think the schools had broken up already. Today, thousands of Teesside families have decided that it is more important for their children to take part in a piece of real local history rather than just learn about it. Just look at their faces, they'll long remember the day they welcomed Juninho to Teesside.'

18TH OCTOBER 2000

According to reports in *The Guardian*, Boro boss Bryan Robson was at the San Siro to run the rule over Croatian international transfer target Zvonimir Boban, who came off the bench as AC Milan drew 3-3 with Barcelona in the Champions League.

18TH OCTOBER 2010

Gordon Strachan quit his role as Middlesbrough manager as he tore up his contract following the club's worst start to a league campaign in two decades. The writing was on the wall days earlier after a 2-1 home loss to Leeds United at the Riverside left Boro two points shy of the Championship relegation spots and prompted chants of 'We want Strachan out' from a large section of the home support.

19TH OCTOBER 1991

Rampaging winger Stuart Ripley was wanted by top-flight Notts County. Meadow Lane manager Neil Warnock was reported to be willing to offer midfielder Phil Turner plus cash for a man Boro boss Lennie Lawrence described as 'the best player in the north-east'. Ultimately, and perhaps wisely, Rippers remained at Boro until the following summer when he switched to Ewood Park, where he went on to win the Premier League in 1995.

20TH OCTOBER 2000

With the final details of the deal complete, former West Bromwich Albion defender Ugo Ehiogu was unveiled as Boro's record £8m signing as he departed Aston Villa for the Riverside.

21ST OCTOBER 1895

The issue of Middlesbrough becoming a larger sporting club was presented to the club's directors when the chairman of the town's baseball club – who also played at the Linthorpe Road Ground – asked if the football club directors would be interested in taking up the management of the baseball club.

21ST OCTOBER 1975

Boro took a huge leap towards cup glory with three second-half goals that handed them a 3-0 win over Mansfield Town in the Anglo-Scottish Cup semi-final first leg. David Armstrong put Jack Charlton's side ahead as he hammered the ball through a crowd of players into the net. With ten minutes remaining John Hickton finished off a pass from Graeme Souness to double the lead and five minutes from time 'Spike' Armstrong added his second and Boro's third when he reacted first after David Mills's shot rebounded off the bar.

STUART RIPLEY WAS THE SUBJECT OF TRANSFER INTEREST FROM NOTTS COUNTY (THE GAZETTE)

21ST OCTOBER 2004

Substitute Stewart Downing struck with 12 minutes remaining to give Middlesbrough a winning start in their UEFA Cup Group E opener against Egaleo in Greece.

22ND OCTOBER 1960

Brian Clough scored his penultimate Boro hat-trick in a chaotic clash at Charlton Athletic that brought an incredible result as both sides scored six goals. Ron Burbeck netted a brace and Derek McLean's strike completed the scoring for Boro as they seemed on course for a high-scoring win until John Sommers equalised for the home side with only a minute remaining.

22ND OCTOBER 2022

Leo Percovich's last match as caretaker boss saw Middlesbrough stumble to a goalless draw against bottom club Huddersfield Town at the Riverside.

23RD OCTOBER 1996

Branco was shown the door by manager Bryan Robson as his spell at Middlesbrough came to an end after less than a year on Teesside with the World Cup winner unable to dislodge favoured left-back Curtis Fleming from the side.

24TH OCTOBER 2022

Michael Carrick completed an on-off move to Middlesbrough to become the new head coach in a return to the club where he had played as a youngster. The 41-year-old was joined at Boro by former defender and head coach Jonathan Woodgate, who took up the role of first-team coach.

25TH OCTOBER 1989

Bruce Rioch blasted bickering in the Boro camp and called for everyone to 'pull together to recapture the spirit and desire we used to possess'. Trailing 1-0 to Wimbledon at half-time at Ayresome Park in the League Cup third round, it seemed as though the call to action had failed to inspire the players. However, a Bernie Slaven goal in the opening minutes of the second half secured a temporary reprieve for Rioch's men as they secured a replay in London, which they lost 1-0 in front of an attendance of just 3,554.

26TH OCTOBER 2010

Club legend Tony Mowbray rejoined Middlesbrough as manager 19 years after swapping Ayresome Park for Parkhead. Replacing Gordon Strachan in the hot seat, at his Riverside unveiling Mogga spoke of his deep connection with, and passion for, the club: 'Since I was six or seven I have been a Middlesbrough fan, so when the opportunity arose – it didn't take me a moment's thought. This is a club I have been passionate about all my life and I have this opportunity to guide them back where they belong. Our ambition is to get the club moving back in the right direction. I have been away for 19 and a half years and every week my phone goes and tells me how Boro did. This is a special place and people who leave Middlesbrough know – you meet Boro people everywhere and they are very passionate about their team because when the Riverside is bouncing it is a special place and we need to get the fans back on board.'

27TH OCTOBER 1998

The national tabloid back pages were dominated by Boro midfielder Paul Gascoigne as he appeared alongside Bryan Robson and declared that he was determined to get his career back on track after a period of treatment in a rehabilitation unit including for alcohol-related challenges.

28TH OCTOBER 2010

The *Evening Gazette* reported that boss Tony Mowbray was battling with Leicester City to sign Ishmael Miller on loan from West Bromwich Albion after the side had notched just 12 goals in the side's 13 opening league matches despite boasting Kris Boyd and Scott McDonald among the forward line.

28TH OCTOBER 2015

Boro enjoyed a famous night in the League Cup at Old Trafford as an impressive rearguard action kept Manchester United's attack at bay for 120 minutes before Aitor Karanka's side triumphed 3-1 on penalties. Tomás Mejías was the hero of the hour, saving from Wayne Rooney and Ashley Young in the shoot-out, in which future Boro boss Michael Carrick hit his penalty over the bar.

29TH OCTOBER 2022

Michael Carrick's first match as head coach ended in defeat at Deepdale. Boro took the lead through a Chuba Akpom close-range header before Emil Riis Jakobsen equalised before the break. In stoppage time Akpom turned hero to villain after conceding the free kick from which Jordan Storey headed home to ensure all three points remained in Lancashire.

30TH OCTOBER 1950

Wilf Mannion and Alex McCrae both scored hat-tricks as Boro trounced visitors Huddersfield Town in a one-sided affair at Ayresome Park. Mannion completed his treble with three first-half goals before McCrae replicated his team-mate's feat in the second half. Johnny Spuhler and Geoff Walker scored the other goals in an 8-0 win that elevated the Teessiders to second place in the top-flight table and just one point off top spot.

30TH OCTOBER 1996

One-time club record signing Nick Barmby signed for Everton in a £5.75m deal that shattered the previous highest fee – £2.3m for Gary Pallister in 1989 – received for a Boro player. Barmby's comments that he had always wanted to play for a big club and that he had joined 'one of the big boys' angered some Middlesbrough supporters but the England international insisted, 'Middlesbrough are a great club, with great fans, and they made my wife and I feel very welcome.'

31ST OCTOBER 1987

Bernie Slaven scored his third Boro hat-trick and Alan Kernaghan notched his side's fourth goal as the ghosts of relegation at Shrewsbury 18 months earlier were laid to rest with a 4-0 Halloween win at Ayresome Park that elevated Bruce Rioch's side to second place in the the Second Division table.

MIDDLESBROUGH
On This Day

NOVEMBER

1ST NOVEMBER 1961

Andy Peake, one of the heroes of Lennie Lawrence's 1991/92 promotion heroes, was born in Market Harborough. Having spent five years together at Charlton Athletic, Lawrence returned to his former club to sign the midfielder in 1991. Peake was voted Middlesbrough's player of the year in the 1992/93 campaign by his team-mates, and remained at Boro for another season until the arrival of Bryan Robson saw his departure from the club. Having turned down the chance to reunite with Lawrence at Bradford City, Peake instead returned to Leicestershire to join the local constabulary.

2ND NOVEMBER 1993

Lennie Lawrence's already threadbare squad was hampered by injuries that left the manager with just nine senior players for the trip to Portsmouth. Michael Barron and Ian Johnson made their debuts while youngsters Mark Taylor and Paul Norton were on the bench as Boro held out until the last 15 minutes when Pompey eventually broke the deadlock through Paul Hall, before John Durnin added a second.

3RD NOVEMBER 1975

Trailing 3-0 from the Anglo-Scottish Cup semi-final first leg at Ayresome Park, any faint hopes that Mansfield might stage an unlikely comeback at Field Mill were dashed as Bobby Murdoch scored four minutes after the break to give the visitors the lead on the night. Graeme Souness made it 5-0 on aggregate late on as Boro progressed to the competition's inaugural final.

4TH NOVEMBER 1995

There were Samba beats on the south bank of the Tees as a sold-out Riverside witnessed new signing Juninho make his debut for Bryan Robson's men against Leeds United. Before kick-off there was a carnival atmosphere with samba drums playing and a sea of yellow and green with many supporters donning the yellow of the Maracanã rather than the red of Middlesbrough. It took the little Brazilian just ten minutes to make an impact on his debut as he ran from his own half and passed several Leeds players before sliding a perfect through pass to Jan Åge Fjørtoft, who chipped the ball over the advancing John Lukic. Unfortunately, Leeds had not read the script and equalised on the stroke of half-time through Brian Deane. In the second half, the 'Little Fella' was booked for a foul on Tony Yeboah before being substituted to a standing ovation.

AFTER A PROMISING START TO THE CAMPAIGN, LENNIE LAWRENCE'S THREADBARE SQUAD FELL TO DEFEAT AT PORTSMOUTH.

4TH **NOVEMBER 2004**

Boro stunned Italian giants Lazio on a memorable UEFA Cup group stage night at the Riverside. Dutch star Bolo Zenden was the home side's hero with a goal in each half in the club's most impressive European performance to date.

5TH **NOVEMBER 2016**

Boro turned in one of their best performances of an otherwise disappointing season as they held Manchester City at the Etihad. Sergio Agüero had put the home side ahead but Aitor Karanka's men fought to stay in the game and were rewarded when against the run of play Dutch midfielder Marten de Roon converted George Friend's cross in stoppage time for a well-earned point.

6TH **NOVEMBER 1950**

Legendary defender George Hardwick swapped the north-east for the north-west as he signed for Oldham Athletic as player-manager. Boro received a fee of £15,000 from the Latics for the former England and Great Britain captain.

6TH **NOVEMBER 1954**

Middlesbrough suffered their heaviest ever defeat as Blackburn Rovers triumphed 9-0 at Ewood Park. The hammering was all the more of a shock given that Boro themselves had hit West Ham for six at Ayresome Park the previous week.

6TH **NOVEMBER 2021**

Middlesbrough parted company with manager Neil Warnock after dropping to 15th in the Championship table following a 1-1 draw at West Bromwich Albion, having won just six games all season.

7TH **NOVEMBER 2021**

One ex-Sheffield United manager was replaced with another at the helm as Chris Wilder succeeded the ousted Neil Warnock. He was joined at the Riverside by long-term right-hand man Alan Knill.

8TH **NOVEMBER 1991**

Long-serving defender Tony Mowbray completed his £1m move to Liam Brady's Glasgow Celtic as he sought a new challenge north of the border after a decade at Ayresome Park. As part of the deal, Middlesbrough would have first refusal should Mowbray depart Parkhead.

9TH NOVEMBER 1997

According to reports in several newspapers, Middlesbrough hoped to sign forward Michele Padovano from Juventus. Despite manager Bryan Robson having been quoted as stating a deal was very close, the Italian attacker never made the move to Teesside after failing to agree personal terms and instead signed for Crystal Palace.

10TH NOVEMBER 1883

Boro's first taste of FA Cup action ended in a 5-1 home defeat to Staveley. With the wind in the Teessiders' favour, the scores were level at half-time at 1-1 but the visitors dominated the second half.

10TH NOVEMBER 1979

Ahead of jetting back to Australia to visit a family member, Craig Johnston scored both goals as John Neal's side produced a fantastic performance against Everton to come away from Goodison Park with a 2-0 win.

11TH NOVEMBER 1899

Joseph Murphy scored Boro's first league hat-trick in what was then Boro's biggest win as a league club as they battered Burton Swifts. Without a league victory since 7 October, George Reid and Charlie Pugh grabbed braces and Geoff Longstaffe a solitary goal as Middlesbrough ran out 8-1 winners at the Linthorpe Road Ground.

11TH NOVEMBER 1975

Boro progressed to the League Cup fifth round after seeing off a battling Peterborough United at Ayresome Park. Stuart Boam scored after only three minutes and despite several chances for both sides, there were no further goals in the first half. The tie was all but over when Boro were awarded a penalty and John Hickton scored from the spot, then just two minutes later David Armstrong put the tie beyond doubt to set up a visit to Burnley.

12TH NOVEMBER 1954

Alan Peacock, who would travel to matchdays after a shift at Cargo Fleet Works on a Saturday morning, signed his first professional contract with the club.

12TH **NOVEMBER 1974**

Jack Charlton had double the reasons to celebrate as Boro knocked Liverpool out of the League Cup at Anfield on the same day he received an OBE from Queen Elizabeth II at Buckingham Palace. In fact, 'Big Jack' almost missed the third-round tie as he made a quick dash from London to Liverpool to make it. For a brief moment in the second half it looked like Bob Paisley's men were certain to progress but Jim Platt produced a fantastic save from Alec Lindsay to keep the scores level. After surviving several Liverpool attacks, in the last minute Boro broke clear and Willie Maddren hit a perfect angled shot past Ray Clemence in the home goal.

12TH **NOVEMBER 1982**

Boro's 'Black Friday' with losses of £12,000 a week saw the club take drastic action as they sacked 15 employees. Malcolm Allison and Cyril Knowles would work together coaching the first team, reserves and juniors under unprecedented pressure.

13TH **NOVEMBER 1982**

Boro recorded their first away win of the season, at Charlton Athletic, as the visitors upstaged home debutant Allan Simonsen, the Danish former European Footballer of the Year who had recently arrived from Barcelona. Captained by new skipper Kevin Beattie, Middlesbrough were impressive throughout and stunned the home side with three goals in the first half without reply. David Shearer opened the scoring after 17 minutes, Mick Kennedy doubled the lead on the half hour and just a minute later Shearer scored his second. The home side improved after the break and when Beattie limped off injured, the Addicks pulled two goals back – including one from their star debutant – but Boro held on for a 3-2 win.

14TH **NOVEMBER 1997**

Having missed out on Michele Padovano, Middlesbrough turned their transfer attention to former player Jaime Moreno. Having impressed for DC United in the USA, Bryan Robson considered a loan deal for the Bolivian international a good attacking option to add to his promotion-chasing squad.

15TH **NOVEMBER 1986**

Following news that the FA had lifted Boro's transfer embargo imposed as a result of debts owed by the previous company, Bernie Slaven made the case for Bruce Rioch not to worry about seeking a new goalscorer as the Scot single-handedly fired Boro to a 3-0 win over Blackpool in the Teessiders' first appearance in the first round of the FA Cup since 1966.

16TH **NOVEMBER 1929**

As storms and fog swept the country, Boro were given a reprieve at Arsenal when, trailing 1-0, referee R.H. Woodward made the decision to abandon the match early in the second half due to the touchlines having become obliterated by mud and rain. The abandonment led to incredible scenes as home captain Tom Parker's protestations to the officials prompted thousands of supporters to climb the barricades and invade the pitch to air their collective grievances. Amid the commotion, a fence collapsed and several people fell down, and even Gunners manager Herbert Chapman's attempts to explain the decision was met with jeers. The baying crowd was only dispersed when the police moved in.

17TH **NOVEMBER 1937**

England won 2-1 against Wales in front of 30,608 at Ayresome Park in the last full England international to be held at the ground. The match generated gate receipts of £2,353 and the second half of the contest was broadcast live on radio across the northern region.

18TH **NOVEMBER 1933**

Despite Sheffield United having taken the lead at Ayresome Park, Boro recorded a stunning 10-3 victory over the Blades. George Camsell scored four goals, Robert Bruce a hat-trick and Bobby Baxter, Charlie Ferguson and Freddie Warren a goal each. Sadly, a combination of inclement November weather and the impact of trade depression meant only 6,461 were in attendance to witness the extraordinary match.

19TH **NOVEMBER 1947**

George Hardwick captained England in their 4-2 win over Sweden at Highbury. Fellow Boro boy Wilf Mannion was at the heart of the action and set up the first goal of Stan Mortensen's hat-trick. He might have scored twice himself had it not been for the fine form of Torsten Lindberg in the visitors' goal.

GEORGE CAMSELL SCORED FOUR TIMES AS BORO WON 10-3 AGAINST SHEFFIELD UNITED AT AYRESOME PARK.

20TH NOVEMBER 1926

It was Fulham's turn to be on the wrong end of a George Camsell masterclass as Ayresome Park's new hero netted four times in a 6-1 win. The victory made it a total of 13 goals for Boro in their two most recent home fixtures and it was the second consecutive time Camsell had scored four goals at home.

21ST NOVEMBER 1998

Defender Dean Gordon scored a second-half screamer from outside the box and Hámilton Ricard recorded his ninth Premier League goal of the season in a 2-0 home win over Coventry City.

22ND NOVEMBER 1947

Boro demolished Blackpool at Ayresome Park with a Wilf Mannion-inspired 4-0 win over the Seasiders. Since dubbed the 'Mannion Match', the 'Golden Boy' did everything but score as Ces McCormack (two), Micky Fenton and Johnny Spuhler grabbed Middlesbrough's goals in the famous win. Mannion later revealed that his performance was inspired by the presence of his fiancée Bernadette in the crowd: 'I was just showing off for my girl Bernadette really. It was her first game – she went along with my brother – and I thought I'd show her what football was about ... I thought it was a bad game really, because I wasn't looking out for the team as much as I usually did, but everyone remembers it as a good game.'

23RD NOVEMBER 1957

Brian Clough scored four of his side's goals in a 5-2 win over Ipswich Town. It was the third time the Grove Hill target man had achieved the feat in the calendar year.

24TH NOVEMBER 1990

Ian Baird scored a hat-trick, Bernie Slaven was also on target, and Robbie Mustoe claimed a late goal against his former club in Boro's 5-2 win over Oxford United at the Manor Ground.

25TH NOVEMBER 2004

Boro tasted defeat in major European competition for the first time as Steve McClaren's much-changed side lost 2-0 at Villarreal, denying them the point required to progress to the knockout stages of the UEFA Cup.

26TH **NOVEMBER 1975**

Boro welcomed the previous season's FA Cup finalists Fulham to Ayresome Park for the first leg of the Anglo-Scottish Cup Final. The home side dominated the first half and David Armstrong and David Mills both spurned good chances. After the break, Jack Charlton's men eventually found a breakthrough and it was Fulham defender Les Strong – who was lucky not to concede a penalty after a coming together with Peter Brine in the box – who proved to be the unlikely source of the goal. Bobby Murdoch played a ball out to Terry Cooper on the left wing, and his cross was met by 'Spike' Armstrong and deflected into the net by the hapless Strong. It proved to be the only goal of the night and gave Charlton's men a slender 1-0 advantage going into the second leg at Craven Cottage a week later.

26TH **NOVEMBER 1988**

The first issue of long-running fanzine *Fly Me To The Moon* went on sale ahead of the Sheffield Wednesday fixture at Ayresome Park. Created by Andi Gilland, Robbie Boal and Tony Pierre on a borrowed typewriter, around 50 copies were published.

27TH **NOVEMBER 1933**

The announcement that the in-form George Camsell would lead the line for England against France the following week prompted shock headlines in the national press given the Framwellgate Moor man's four-year absence from the national side.

27TH **NOVEMBER 1996**

A Juninho-inspired Middlesbrough stunned north-east rivals Newcastle United in the League Cup with a 3-1 win at the Riverside. Steve Vickers and Derek Whyte were the unlikely source of the opening goal with the latter turning in a drilled cross-shot by his defensive partner. Alan Shearer equalised for Kevin Keegan's men on the stroke of half-time with a header from a Keith Gillespie corner. Just after the hour, Emerson, Juninho and Fabrizio Ravanelli combined to set up Danish international Mikkel Beck, who turned the Italian's pass into the net from inside the six-yard box. In the last minute Juninho tormented the Magpies' defence before crossing for Ravanelli to bundle home his 16th goal in 17 games for his new club.

28TH NOVEMBER 2015

Adam Clayton scored against his old club after just nine minutes and Emilio Nsue made sure of victory with six minutes remaining in a vital victory for Aitor Karanka's men at Huddersfield Town that propelled Boro into the Championship play-offs ahead of Derby County on goal difference.

29TH NOVEMBER 1947

An unchanged Boro side crossed the Pennines to take on Blackburn Rovers at Ewood Park and produced an outstanding performance to secure a 7-1 victory which was not only their record Football League away win but also Rovers' heaviest home defeat for almost six decades.

30TH NOVEMBER 1985

Boro leapfrogged opponents Shrewsbury Town in the league following their 3-1 win courtesy of goals from Gary Rowell, Pat Heard and Tony McAndrew. Middlesbrough's third league home win of the season attracted a gate of just 4,061 at Ayresome Park, at the time the second-lowest league crowd in the ground's history.

MIDDLESBROUGH
On This Day

DECEMBER

1st DECEMBER 1990

A glaring first-half miss by Andy Payton ensured Middlesbrough and struggling Hull City went in level at half-time at Ayresome Park before goals from Ian Baird, Bernie Slaven and Paul Kerr saw the home side eventually overpower the Tigers. The result moved Colin Todd's men up to third in the Second Division and left Stan Ternent's Hull languishing in 23rd.

2nd DECEMBER 1967

Boro doubled their away wins for the season after coming out on top of a high-scoring game at the Baseball Ground. John O'Rourke scored his third Boro hat-trick and John Hickton added the visitors' other goal in a 4-2 win over Derby County.

3rd DECEMBER 1910

A 1-0 home defeat of Sunderland at Ayresome Park ultimately proved to be a match that engulfed Middlesbrough in a football scandal that would gain national coverage and bring FA condemnation. With the general election voting scheduled to begin two days after the fixture, it was felt that Boro chairman and Conservative candidate Thomas Gibson Poole's chances of success at the ballot box would be improved with a win over his team's rivals. Manager Andy Walker was sent to offer bribes to Sunderland players – including £10 to Roker Park captain Charlie Thomson. The Sunderland chairman was eventually informed and the matter was reported to the FA. Gibson Poole and Walker were given life bans, despite a 12,500-strong petition to the FA to revoke Walker's punishment. As for the election, the Liberal candidate Penry Williams stormed home with 10,313 votes compared to the disgraced Gibson Poole's 6,568 votes.

3rd DECEMBER 1968

Boro went joint-top of the Second Division with an impressive 4-1 win over Bristol City at Ayresome Park. John Hickton ended a near three-month goal drought with a brace, with Derrick Downing and Eric McMordie adding the other goals for Stan Anderson's promotion-chasers.

3rd DECEMBER 1991

Brilliant Boro progressed to the quarter-finals of the League Cup at the expense of high-flying top-flight outfit Manchester City. After a goalless first half in the fog at Ayresome Park, Robbie Mustoe gave Boro the lead in the 57th minute and Paul Wilkinson doubled the advantage 12 minutes later. David White struck late to offer some hope to the Maine Road side but Boro held on.

4TH **DECEMBER 1935**

George Camsell scored a brace as England beat Germany 3-0 at White Hart Lane. The match brought 10,000 German supporters to London, and it proved controversial as swastikas flew at the home of a club with strong Jewish heritage; ahead of kick-off the visiting team made Nazi salutes. Former England star Charlie Buchan hailed Camsell as the standout performer and 'Hero of the Match' in what he considered an otherwise disappointing forward line as he criticised Stanley Matthews and felt Cliff Bastin – who scored the game's other goal – held the ball far too long.

4TH **DECEMBER 2000**

In an unprecedented move, Bryan Robson stepped aside as Boro boss and former England manager Terry Venables' on-off move to the Riverside as head coach was confirmed. 'El Tel' brought proven pedigree to Teesside as a former Barcelona and Spurs manager who had also coached at international level. Having agreed a short-term deal until the end of the season, Venables would work alongside Robbo as the club attempted to stave off the threat of relegation. The move proved to be ingenious as Venables inspired a huge turnaround in form and Boro stayed up relatively comfortably.

5TH **DECEMBER 1992**

Craig Hignett made his Boro debut after joining from Crewe Alexandra, and John Hendrie made club history when he scored their first Premier League hat-trick in a 3-2 win over Blackburn Rovers. The Lancashire outfit were condemned to their first away defeat of the season despite having led through a Jason Wilcox goal before Hendrie stole the show. It was, however, a nervy win for Boro as they were forced to hang on after a Jimmy Phillips own goal.

6TH **DECEMBER 1933**

Returning to the international fold after four years away, it took George Camsell just 12 minutes to get on the scoresheet as he scored two goals in England's 4-1 win over France at White Hart Lane. Camsell's first goal came after he drove through the defence before smashing a shot into the top-left corner of the net. England added another goal through Eric Brook before Camsell made it 3-0 with an extraordinary effort from near the corner flag that swerved on to the crossbar and dropped over the line. Despite his brace, Camsell once again found himself in the international wilderness and did not play for England again until December 1935.

7TH DECEMBER 1996

AWOL Brazilian star Emerson was in the headlines as it was reported that the midfielder was set to make a return to Middlesbrough with his wife, who had been ill, after he had remained in South America with her.

8TH DECEMBER 1894

Boro fought back from trailing at half-time to record their biggest away league victory of the season as they ran out 4-1 winners at Bishop Auckland en route to another Northern League title.

9TH DECEMBER 1939

Boro recorded their first home win in the North East Regional League – established owing to the suspension of the national leagues due to the Second World War – in a 3-1 victory over Halifax Town. Micky Fenton, Bill Forrest and George Camsell got the goals in front of a then-record low gate of just 1,200 as debates raged on over whether football should continue in war conditions and supporters showed apathy towards the regional leagues.

10TH DECEMBER 1938

Blackpool were battered by a Wilf Mannion-inspired Boro at Ayresome Park in a 9-2 win for Wilf Gillow's side. Not to be confused with the famous 'Mannion Match' against the Seasiders nine years later, the result came as something of a surprise after the Teessiders' form had stuttered with only one win in the previous five matches. It took the home side just four minutes to get off the mark with Mannion opening the scoring as the deluge began. By half-time Middlesbrough led 5-0 courtesy of a hat-trick from the 'Golden Boy' and goals from Cliff Chadwick and the ever-reliable Micky Fenton. The second half largely continued in the vein of the first with Mannion adding a fourth, Fenton grabbing two more to complete his own hat-trick and Chadwick notching once more to claim a brace. Despite two second-half goals from Blackpool, it was Boro's day.

11TH DECEMBER 1973

Middlesbrough went five points clear at the top of the Second Division with a comfortable 3-0 win over Preston North End at Ayresome Park in front of 23,980, the biggest crowd of the season to date. The 'Battle of the Charltons' – with Jack's brother Bobby in the opposition dugout – was a one-sided affair. Boro almost took the lead after nine minutes when John Hickton burst through but debutant Ron Healey made a brave save and had to leave the field for treatment with former Manchester United star David Sadler temporarily standing in as goalkeeper. Within six minutes the centre-half conceded as David Mills fired home and even with Healey back between the sticks, the visitors fell two goals behind as Bobby Murdoch fired in a 25-yard thunderbolt. In the last minute, Graeme Souness added Boro's third with what reporter Eric Paylor described as 'the best goal of the game' as the Scot ruthlessly fired past the hapless Healey to give the result the more convincing scoreline their attacking play had warranted.

12TH DECEMBER 1964

Boro completed their first double of the season as they triumphed 4-1 over Southampton at Ayresome Park following on from an opening-day victory at The Dell. Jimmy Irvine put the home side ahead after five minutes but Terry Paine equalised after 31 minutes. Don Mason restored the advantage seven minutes later and after spurning a couple of chances, Boro eventually increased their lead in the 76th minute through Arthur Kaye's penalty. James Townsend added a fourth for Raich Carter's men with seven minutes remaining to put some gloss on the scoreline.

13TH DECEMBER 1997

Boro left it late to see off their upcoming League Cup opponents Reading at the Riverside as braces from Mikkel Beck and Craig Hignett flattered them with a 4-0 win. Although the home side had enjoyed the better of the contest, it was not until 13 minutes from time that Hignett's goal opened the Royals' floodgates down by the River Tees.

14TH DECEMBER 1997

The People reported that Bryan Robson had made an ambitious 'take it or leave it' £4.5m bid for Everton's former Glasgow Rangers target man Duncan Ferguson, although Goodison Park boss Howard Kendall was reluctant to let the striker leave Merseyside.

15TH DECEMBER 1995

The *Hartlepool Mail* reported that the arrival of Brazilian Footballer of the Year Juninho in Middlesbrough had not just brought excitement for Boro fans but also brought an unexpected boost to tourism, having provoked a massive demand for information on the town.

16TH DECEMBER 1978

Despite giving Chelsea a goal start through Peter Osgood, John Neal's side subsequently dismantled the bottom-of-the-table Blues as they ran out 7-2 winners. Mark Proctor equalised just four minutes after Osgood's opener and on 36 minutes Micky Burns scored the first of his four goals of the afternoon. Two minutes later Burns added his second and Boro's third. After the break David Armstrong made it four and despite John Bumstead pulling one back for the Londoners, Burns restored the three-goal advantage then with 15 minutes remaining Terry Cochrane scored the goal of the game. With the Holgate chanting 'we want seven', Burns duly obliged with a minute remaining to become the first Boro player to score four goals in a top-flight fixture since Micky Fenton managed the same feat against Stoke City in 1946.

17TH DECEMBER 1966

John O'Rourke and Arthur Horsfield both scored braces against fellow bottom-half side Colchester United in a 4-0 win at Ayresome Park.

18TH DECEMBER 1937

Future club legend George Hardwick made a disastrous start to his Boro debut as he scored an own goal in the opening minutes in a 2-1 Ayresome Park defeat to Bolton Wanderers.

18TH DECEMBER 1994

Boro trounced Burnley 3-0 at Turf Moor in a match screened live on regional TV. John Hendrie completed his hat-trick in the 93rd minute to take his tally against the Clarets to five goals in two games. The victory put Boro top of the First Division over Christmas as Bryan Robson's men pushed for promotion in his first season as manager.

JOHN HENDRIE WAS THE HAT-TRICK HERO IN BORO'S 3-0 WIN OVER BURNLEY AT TURF MOOR.

19TH DECEMBER 1998

Boro's final pre-Christmas fixture produced one of the finest away victories in the club's history as the newly promoted side stunned title-chasing Manchester United in another five-goal thriller. Boro stormed into a 2-0 first-half lead courtesy of Hámilton Ricard and Dean Gordon strikes. Just before the hour Brian Deane capitalised on a mix-up in the United defence to put Boro 3-0 up and with it send the travelling faithful delirious. As the supporters sang 'We're going to win the league', Manchester United hit back with two goals in eight minutes but Boro hung on to gain a famous win at Old Trafford.

19TH DECEMBER 2015

Aitor Karanka described José Mourinho as Boro's lucky charm with the recently deposed former Chelsea boss in attendance to support his former Real Madrid assistant's Middlesbrough side as they stunned the Amex Stadium with a 3-0 win. Goals from Kike, Albert Adomah and Cristhian Stuani ended Brighton's unbeaten start to the league campaign. After the match, Mourinho visited the Boro dressing room to congratulate the side as they looked forward to Christmas topping the Championship table.

20TH DECEMBER 1980

John Neal named an unchanged team for the visit of Spurs to Ayresome Park and the good understanding built up between his players was apparent from the off as David Armstrong crossed and David Hodgson headed Boro into the lead after just five minutes. Spurs equalised within a minute but the home side were not to be deterred and after 11 minutes Hodgson combined with David Shearer before receiving the ball back and firing his team back into the lead. On the hour Hodgson scored the first hat-trick of his senior career when he headed in a Craig Johnston cross. The Australian then went from provider to goalscorer as he netted his 11th goal of the season to secure a 4-1 win.

21ST DECEMBER 1968

A three-goal win at Craven Cottage ensured the gap between Stan Anderson's men and table-topping Derby County was just one point going into Christmas. Despite Fulham being the basement club of the Second Division, they put up a valiant fight against the promotion-chasers from the north-east. It was not until the 70th minute that the home defence was breached when Derrick Downing scored from a John Hickton cross. A minute later the roles were reversed and Hickton duly headed home a Downing cross to double Boro's lead and end the game as a contest. It was not the end of Hickton's goalscoring, however, as with one minute remaining the Chesterfield-born marksman scored his second of the game.

21ST DECEMBER 1996

Middlesbrough's scheduled match with Blackburn Rovers was called off with dramatic consequences. The previous day, with a squad decimated with injuries and illness and with a virus sweeping through the camp that meant club doctors were unable to determine how many more players would be impacted overnight, Middlesbrough notified the Premier League of the dire situation. Despite believing they had reached an agreement with the league's officials to play the match at a future date, Boro were ultimately docked three points for not fulfilling the fixture.

21ST DECEMBER 1998

Bernie Slaven's buttocks were the star attraction for Christmas shoppers as the former Boro striker was good to his word that he would bare his backside in the window of the town's Binns department store if Bryan Robson's men won at Old Trafford. Some 2,000 were estimated to have turned out in the town centre two days after the shock 3-2 victory over Manchester United.

22ND DECEMBER 1959

Boro were dealt a huge festive blow when outside-right Billy Day broke his leg in a tackle against team-mate Micky McNeil in a practice match. The injury and subsequent setbacks ruled Day out of first-team action until February 1961.

23RD DECEMBER 1967

A crumbling Carlisle defence ensured the majority of the 27,952 crowd – the highest of the season to date – left Ayresome Park in festive spirits as John O'Rourke scored a second-half hat-trick and Mike Kear added another to complete a 4-0 victory and make it five consecutive wins with their first victory over the Cumbrians.

23RD DECEMBER 2017

Garry Monk was dismissed as Middlesbrough manager despite his side having fought back from a goal down to win 2-1 at Sheffield Wednesday. Despite significant expenditure, Monk oversaw just four wins in Middlesbrough's first 13 league games, although the club had improved to win six of their next ten to move within three points of the play-off places.

BERNIE SLAVEN BARED HIS BUTTOCKS IN BINNS' WINDOW AFTER VOWING TO DO SO IF BORO WON AT OLD TRAFFORD.

24TH DECEMBER 1889

The result was academic but provided Christmas Eve cheer for the Linthorpe Road faithful as Middlesbrough dealt Edinburgh University a footballing lesson, scoring eight goals without reply in the first of their holiday friendly fixtures.

25TH DECEMBER 1926

Flying high in the second tier and with their young talisman George Camsell topping the Second Division's goalscoring charts, Boro had every reason to be optimistic as they crossed the Pennines to take on Manchester City at Maine Road on Christmas Day 1926, not least with Camsell in fine form having hit four against Swansea City the previous week. Yet visits to the blue side of the 'Cottonopolis' had proven fruitless for Boro, who had not recorded an away win at City in their league history. With Boro going a goal down in the opening minute, it looked like the bleak run was going to continue until Camsell sprang into action. The former Durham City forward grabbed the equaliser with a goal that appeared offside, before giving the visitors a 2-1 half-time lead after Goodchild in the home goal spilled Billy Pease's effort. A topsy-turvy second half followed as the Citizens equalised before Camsell daringly headed his hat-trick goal from a Pease cross to restore Boro's lead before City once again drew level. Not satisfied with a point and with Camsell wanting to add to his hat-trick, the forward converted Williams' assist to put Boro ahead once more before getting his 'reward for a purely individual dash between the backs' to give the visitors a 5-3 win.

26TH DECEMBER 1996

Boxing Day brought a six-goal thriller at the Riverside with Everton who included Nick Barmby, their recent signing from Boro, among their ranks. The first half saw the two sides go in level at 2-2 after goals from Craig Hignett and Clayton Blackmore were cancelled out on each occasion through a David Unsworth penalty and Duncan Ferguson header. The second half belonged to Juninho as the Brazilian star scored two goals and Boro recorded their first league victory since winning at Goodison Park in September.

GEORGE CAMSELL SCORED FIVE GOALS AGAINST MANCHESTER CITY ON CHRISTMAS DAY (GREENMON COLLECTION

27TH DECEMBER 1926

After George Camsell had scored all five of Boro's goals in a 5-3 win at Maine Road two days earlier, the Ayresome Park festive fixture brought a record attendance and extraordinary scenes. For those unable to find space on the terraces, the roof of the old stand at Ayresome Park – relocated from the club's former Linthorpe Road Ground in 1903 – endured the strain of dozens of supporters keen to see the great Camsell in action for themselves, with the local press describing fans as 'on the roof of the world at Ayresome Park' and how 'human beings appeared to alight on the tiles like birds'. The *North Eastern Daily Gazette* captured the record-breaking moment: 'The history of the Middlesbrough Football Club affords no precedent to the scenes at Ayresome Park yesterday. A holiday crowd of 44,000 was admitted – 6,000 more than the previous record – and many more were turned away. So great was the crush that probably 8,000 or 10,000 swarmed over the barriers, but controlled only by a handful of police they were perfectly orderly.' The fans were not left disappointed as, quite remarkably, Camsell bagged a brace to make it seven goals in 48 hours and, despite the visitors getting a goal and pushing for an equaliser, his efforts secured a significant win for Middlesbrough. At the full-time whistle, many of those crowded along the touchline flooded on to the pitch to greet their heroes. As the man of the hour, Camsell was chaired on the shoulders of supporters from the hallowed Ayresome pitch to the dressing room as the Boro faithful hailed Framwellgate Moor's finest.

27TH DECEMBER 1949

The majority of the ground attendance record 53,802 fans packed into Ayresome Park departed delighted after a solitary Alex McCrae strike secured a 1-0 win for Boro over north-east rivals Newcastle United.

28TH DECEMBER 2015

Cristhian Stuani's opening-minute goal against Sheffield Wednesday at the Riverside Stadium was enough to send Middlesbrough back to the top of the Championship. The Uruguayan netted after just 44 seconds as he tapped in from a Stewart Downing cross. The Middlesbrough defence withstood an Owls onslaught to record a club record-equalling seventh successive league shutout.

EVERTON'S NICKY BARMBY ENDURED AN UNHAPPY RETURN TO THE RIVERSIDE AS JUNINHO-INSPIRED BORO RAN OUT 4-2 WINNERS.

29TH DECEMBER 1894

Boro recorded a 13-0 home win over North Skelton Rovers at the Linthorpe Road Ground as they showed no mercy to their East Cleveland rivals, who played the match with only ten men. John Gettins scored a hat-trick, Alf Nelmes notched a brace and Dave Mullen added the other home goal before the break. Things went from bad to worse for Rovers as the Teessiders netted another seven goals. A. Rodger scored two, Gettings scored his fourth, Nelmes completed his hat-trick, Mullen took his tally to a brace while Pearson and Wilson also added their names to the scoresheet.

29TH DECEMBER 1973

Middlesbrough made club history with a 2-0 victory over Crystal Palace that extended their unbeaten league record to 22 games. Two quickfire goals midway through the first half from Alan Foggon and David Armstrong were enough to secure the win as Charlton's side ended the year as record breakers and led the Second Division table.

30TH DECEMBER 1911

Middlesbrough headed into 1912 placed sixth in the First Division after ending their year with a barnstorming 3-3 draw with Sunderland at Ayresome Park. George Elliott gave the home side the lead after ten minutes but the visitors pulled level before half-time. The second half followed a similar pattern with Billy James restoring Boro's advantage after 57 minutes but Sunderland fought back and took the lead before Edmund 'Ninty' Eyre scored a last-gasp equaliser.

STEWART DOWNING SET UP CRISTHIAN STUANI'S OPENING MINUTE GOAL AGAINST SHEFFIELD WEDNESDAY THAT GAVE BORO A 1-0 WIN.

31ST DECEMBER 1960

New Year's Eve 1960 was one to forget for Liverpool after Brian Clough showed no goodwill to the Merseyside men as he scored a dramatic winner at Anfield. Boro opened the scoring in bizarre fashion when John Molyneux played a back-pass to Bert Slater who slipped and the ball bounced into the unguarded net. Alan Peacock doubled the visitors' lead when heading in from a free kick, but the Merseysiders pulled a goal back almost immediately through Alan A'Court, whose cross ended up deceiving Middlesbrough stopper Bob Appleby. Kevin Lewis equalised before the break for Liverpool, with Appleby injured in the process as he collided with the woodwork. With the keeper receiving treatment for a broken nose, left-back Mick McNeil stood in for his team-mate between the sticks. Appleby bravely rejoined the fray but was again picking the ball out of the net when Lewis scored his second to give the home side the lead for the first time. It was not until 12 minutes from time that Boro equalised through Clough capitalising on a mix-up in defence, and ten minutes later his volley with just two minutes remaining ensured Middlesbrough ended 1960 on a high with a 4-3 victory.

ALAN PEACOCK WAS AMONGST THE SCORERS IN MIDDLESBROUGH'S DRAMATIC 4-3 WIN AT ANFIELD.

SELECTED BIBLIOGRAPHY

Allan, D., Bell, G., Glasper, H., & Walker, M., *Who's That Team They Call the Boro: the Essential History of Middlesbrough Football Club* (2003: Middlesbrough FC, Newton Aycliffe)

Glasper, H., *Middlesbrough: A Complete Record* (1993: Breedon, Derby)

Glasper, H., & Kershaw, C., *The Boro Bible: A Complete History of Middlesbrough Football Club* (1999: Middlesbrough FC, Newton Aycliffe)

Paylor, E., *Middlesbrough Football Club* (1989: Archive Publications, Manchester)

Paylor, E., & Wilson, J., *Ayresome Park Memories: 20th Anniversary Edition* (2004: DB Publishing, Brentford)

Matthews, T., *Middlesbrough FC Miscellany* (2014: Amberley, Stroud)

Varley, N., *Golden Boy: A Biography of Wilf Mannion* (1997: Aurum Press, London)